MOUNTAIN MOVERS

A series of Studies by

Dr Ken Chant

COPYRIGHT © 1995 BY KEN CHANT. ALL RIGHTS RESERVED WORLDWIDE.

VISION CHRISTIAN COLLEGE

P.O. BOX 577 KINGSWOOD NSW 2747, AUSTRALIA

ISBN 1 875577 02 5 PUBLISHED BY KEN CHANT MINISTRIES

Contents

POSSESS YOUR POSSESSIONS!...7

HOW TO PLEASE GOD!..17

GOD'S MIGHTY PROMISES..25

HOW TO BE MADE WHOLE!..33

WHEN THE PROMISE FAILS..43

POWERFUL PRAYER...51

WHY PEOPLE DON'T PRAY...61

PART ONE - THINGS THAT HINDER PRAYER.....................................63

PART TWO - BEYOND PAGAN PRAYER..71

PRAISE YOUR WAY TO VICTORY!...81

NO SWEAT!..91

MUCH, MUCH MORE!...103

THE KEYS OF THE KINGDOM!..113

REIGNING AS KINGS!..121

MOUNTAIN MOVERS..131

A NOTE ON GENDER
It is unfortunate that the English language does not contain an adequate generic pronoun (especially in the singular number) that includes without bias both male and female. So "he, him, his, man, mankind," with their plurals, must do the work for both sexes. Accordingly, wherever it is appropriate to do so in the following pages, please include the feminine gender in the masculine, and vice versa.

FOOTNOTES
A work once fully referenced will thereafter be noted either by "ibid" or "op. cit."

ABBREVIATIONS
Abbreviations commonly used for the books of the Bible are

Genesis	Ge		Nahum	Na
Exodus	Ex		Habakkuk	Hb
Leviticus	Le		Zephaniah	Zp
Numbers	Nu		Haggai	Hg
Deuteronomy	De		Zechariah	Zc
Joshua	Js		Malachi	Mal
Judges	Jg		Matthew	Mt
Ruth	Ru		Mark	Mk
1 Samuel	1 Sa		Luke	Lu
2 Samuel	2 Sa		John	Jn
1 Kings	1 Kg		Acts	Ac
2 Kings	2 Kg		Romans	Ro
1 Chronicles	1 Ch		1 Corinthians	1 Co
2 Chronicles	2 Ch		2 Corinthians	2 Co
Ezra	Ezr		Galatians	Ga
Nehemiah	Ne		Ephesians	Ep
Esther	Es		Philippians	Ph
Job	Jb		Colossians	Cl
Psalm	Ps		1 Thessalonians	1 Th
Proverbs	Pr		2 Thessalonians	2 Th
Ecclesiastes	Ec		1 Timothy	1 Ti
Song of Songs	Ca *		2 Timothy	2 Ti
Isaiah	Is		Titus	Tit
Jeremiah	Je		Philemon	Phm
Lamentations	La		Hebrews	He
Ezekiel	Ez		James	Ja
Daniel	Da		1 Peter	1 Pe
Hosea	Ho		2 Peter	2 Pe
Joel	Jl		1 John	1 Jn
Amos	Am		2 John	2 Jn

Obadiah	Ob	3 John	3 Jn
Jonah	Jo	Jude	Ju
Micah	Mi	Revelation	Re

- *Ca is an abbreviation of Canticles, a derivative of the Latin name of the Song of Solomon, which is sometimes also called the Song of Songs.

POSSESS YOUR POSSESSIONS!

> *"Then the house of Jacob shall possess their own possessions"*
> *(Obadiah, verse 17).*

What a strange expression! How can you "possess" what you already possess?

The prophet is thinking about Israel. That nation had received some stunning promises from God (for example, Deuteronomy 28:9-13). What astonishing prosperity God offered Israel! In the mind of God, everything he had promised already belonged to the people, but they had never seized their inheritance. Sometimes through unbelief, sometimes through cowardice, sometimes through ignorance, or for another reason, they had left the splendid promise of God unclaimed. But one day, said Obadiah, that will all change, and Israel will at last fully possess its own possessions.

The church is like Israel. God has given us immense benefits. Christians are the owners of those blessings, yet they don't possess them. We live as though our property were not ours, as though we still have to buy God's gracious gifts by our own works, as though they have to be earned instead of received joyfully by faith.

This opening chapter does two things: it presents three of the benefits that we Christians are called upon to "possess" by faith; and it lays a foundation for the chapters that follow, for the basic theme of this book is how you, by faith, can "possess your own possessions!"

POSSESS YOUR RIGHT TO PARDON

Christians often receive forgiveness from God without going on to grasp boldly his full pardon. They know they have escaped the penalty of sin, yet they walk in apprehension, sure that God still remembers every fault, and that he is unwilling to restore them to his full favor. Indeed, it takes a certain tenacity of faith, a certain aggressiveness of spirit, to possess the complete pardon, the full restoration, that the Father freely offers us in Christ.

Why?

Simply because every time you step up to the throne, and begin to ask God for some great thing, some mighty miracle, your own conscience (with some assistance from the Accuser) will stand in your way. A voice will whisper in your ear: "Who do you think you are? What right do you have to approach God like this? How dare you ask God for such a splendid gift! Don't you remember how roughly you spoke to your wife this morning?" And so on ... the list of accusations grows, the remembrance of your guilt intensifies, until you stammer an apology to God for having the effrontery ever to come before him with anything but tears! You cannot imagine how you had the gall to suppose you ever deserved anything from the Father except stern discipline!

But hear what God thinks about the matter: Psalm 103:12; Isaiah 44:22; Hebrews 8:12; and Jeremiah 50:20, which says, "search will be made for your sins, but none will be found." *Why won't they be found? See Micah 7:18-19. How hard it is to find something that has been buried at sea! Those who hunt for shipwrecks often know the exact location where a vessel once sank, yet they cannot find it. The shifting tides and sand do their work well and swallow into oblivion the ships and treasure that fall under their power.*

Personal victory, bold access to the throne of grace, authority in prayer, your right to great answers from God, all begin here; that is, with an unwavering assurance that by the Blood of Jesus all memory of your sin has been erased, and that you can come freely before God as his faultless child (Hebrews 4:16; 10:19-23). Do not be denied. Possess your pardon!

Take time also to read the following promises - 1 John 1:9-10; 2:1-2; Titus 2:14; Hebrews 9:14; Revelation 1:5-6; 5:9-10; and many others. Those references all declare in different ways that God has utterly destroyed, not only our sins, but also all evidence of that sin, and even the very memory of it! There is a poetic license in such statements. It is plain that neither God nor we can literally forget that we have sinned. But the scripture is graphically showing how God is ready to behave toward us as if we had never sinned. In response, he expects us to put the memory of sin out of our minds, and by the Blood of Christ to come freely into his presence.

Note also how the apostle, in Hebrews 6:1, instructs us not to keep on repenting over sins that have already been the subject of repentance. Don't let Satan block your access to the throne of God by constantly stirring up the memory of sin. When God forgives, he forgets, and is willing to deal with you as if you never had violated any of his commands.

Because of Calvary, you have a right to affirm, "Search may be made for my sins, but none will be found! I stand forgiven and restored to the favor of God."

POSSESS YOUR RIGHT TO PROVISION

See Ephesians 1:3. Note that God has already blessed you with "every spiritual blessing" in the heavenlies. The phrase "spiritual blessings" does not mean "spiritual" in contrast with "physical", nor "heavenly" in contrast with "earthly". It does not describe some ethereal joy that we might hope to gain on the other side of the grave. Rather, it means every blessing, every promise, every gift, that God has already laid up for us in Christ, in the heavenlies, which the Holy Spirit will convey into our lives when we boldly seize the promise by faith. It means personal victory, bodily healing, financial supply, successful service, and a hundred other priceless benefits that are yours now in Christ, waiting for you to possess them!

The annals of Alexander the Great provide an analogy to the generosity of our King. The Macedonian general had learned that many of his soldiers were heavily in debt to the merchants and moneylenders of Babylon. This burden had begun to erode the morale of his army, so although their own extravagance had impoverished them, Alexander decided to pay their debts out of his own treasury. The men, however, feared that they were being tested, to separate the wastrels from the frugal, and they showed reluctance to make their needs known. Alexander recognized the cause of their tardiness, that it was shame not stubbornness, so he ordered the entire army to be paraded before him. When they were assembled, he set up a line of tables, and piled onto them a vast sum of gold coins, then bade the men to come and claim what they needed. They pressed forward eagerly, and all their debts were cleared by the king's generosity.

We are like the soldiers in that story. The same two things that held back Alexander's troops also inhibit many Christians from possessing God's provision

- they are ashamed. Just as the soldiers knew that their debt was a product of their own folly, and that they deserved censure rather than rescue, so many Christians feel that it is presumptuous for them to ask God to help them out of their financial troubles. "It's my own fault," they say; "it's too late now to beg for help, I should have been more careful. Now I must learn to live with this problem and patiently endure the results of my carelessness." But that self-deprecating attitude denies the promises of God. No doubt the Lord wants to teach you wisdom, and he wants to help you to avoid repeating your mistakes. No doubt he wants to teach us all how to be good stewards of the resources he has given us. He might even have to chastise you if you are willfully disobedient (Hebrews 12:5-11). But he will never forsake you (13:5-6). Help is always available. Be bold to claim that help (Matthew 6:25-34).

- they are timid. Just as the soldiers were afraid that Alexander was tricking them into admitting their fault, so that he could punish them, so many Christians are afraid that God will be angry with them if they confess their needs and ask for miraculous provision. Unhappily, multitudes of people have been indoctrinated to think that true piety is passive before God, asking nothing, wanting nothing, content to accept whatever "Providence" has appointed. They have been taught that it is arrogant, even irreligious, to expect great things from God. Yet when you turn to scripture you will find yourself confronted by the demand: "Come boldly to the throne, and ask for grace and mercy to help in time of need!" (Hebrews 4:16; 10:19-23; etc.) No more than Alexander did from his troops does God want your excuses or apologies; he looks instead for you to show confidence in his promise and boldness to seize the best of his blessing.

So then, there are two kinds of timidity that may affect us when we need to ask God for money (or for any kind of miracle of divine supply). One is a healthy caution, based on respect for such scriptures as Matthew 6:24; Luke 16:10-15; and 1 Timothy 6:6-10. We must certainly let those scriptures measure our attitude toward money; and we need to be content with whatever level of affluence best reflects the purpose of God for each of our lives (some may be called to great wealth, others to comparative poverty). The other is unhealthy. Based on cringing guilt, it reflects deep-seated unbelief and a sorry failure to understand the measure of God's kindness toward us in Christ. It shows a twisted sense of unworthiness, a false humility, spiritual cowardice, disgraceful reluctance to accept the Word of God. Sometimes it results from listening to the devil's lies; sometimes from a carnal wish, by suffering deprivation, to make a kind of personal atonement for sin. It may also be an expression of sheer pride, a determination to "make it by myself" without God's help, which disguises itself in downcast humility. Whatever the reason, timidity is forbidden to the Christian who approaches the throne of God! (Hebrews 4:16; 10:19-23).

Timorous souls need to become subject to the empowering Spirit (Acts 1:8); to gain a revelation of the promises of God (Ephesians 1:16-19); to stir up the implanted grace of God (2 Timothy 1:6-7); to begin to behave as children of God should (Romans 8:14-17); to stand tall in the courage of a servant of God (1 Corinthians 15:58; 16:13).

If you want further encouragement to trust God to meet your need, then ponder these promises: Matthew 6:25-34; Luke 6:38; 12:22-31; 2 Corinthians 8:8-9; 9:6-11; Philippians 4:19 (note how this promise sits within a framework of monetary gifts, verses 15-18); Proverbs 11:24-25; Hosea 14:4-7; Ephesians 3:20; plus every other promise of answered prayer in the Bible.

Are there any conditions attached to getting such prayers answered? Yes, there are. At least three conditions must be met:

    (1)   *God does not hear those who are willfully continuing in sin;*

(2) *God will be as generous toward us as we are toward him (within the limits of our resources);*

(3) *perfunctory giving will not activate the promise - rather, your gift must be accompanied by faith, gladly confident that God will richly supply all your needs.*

Before we leave the story of Alexander, notice that his motives were not entirely altruistic; generosity was not his sole reason. A large measure of self-interest lay behind his kindness to his soldiers. That dispirited body of men were worthless to him. But Alexander's magnanimity fired them with a new zeal; their enthusiasm and toughness were wonderfully restored. Likewise, God needs a devoted, powerful, aggressive band of warriors, well-equipped for battle. So away with that spurious shame, that tedious timidity. Grip the pardon and provision of your God, and armed for war, go out and win victories for the King!

POSSESS YOUR RIGHT TO A PHYSICIAN

Just as surely as the Bible is full of promises of pardon and provision, so it is full of promises of healing. Turn where you will, and you will find that sickness is contrary to the best purpose of God, that his highest wish is for his people to enjoy good health (Exodus 15:26; Deuteronomy 7:15; Psalm 103:3; etc.)

Why then are some not healed when they pray? Because we have to possess the promise of healing; it will not fall into your hand of its own accord; you must make it happen by faith.

Have you asked God to make you well? Does he seem to ignore you? This is not the time to abandon hope, nor to surrender your trust in the covenant of healing. Rather, you should be like the people Jesus "passed by" in the gospels, but who refused to be denied their miracle. Have you ever noticed those stories? Jesus was apparently willing to walk straight past many people who were sick or troubled, without making any attempt to help them. The gospels imply that he would have gone on his way, ignoring them, if they had not found a way to arrest his attention. Consider the following -

> *Matthew 9:27. The Greek expression used here has the sense, "he had left that place, and had no intention of returning to it." Indeed, so determined was Jesus to go on, he ignored the cries of the blind men who came stumbling after him, until they had forced their way into the house. Only then did he give any attention to their demand for healing.*

Matthew 20:30. The Greek expression is the same as before. Notice how Jesus walked right past those blind men (so far as we can tell) without even throwing them a small coin. When he was finally stopped by their insistent shouts, he still made them come to him instead of him walking back to them - which would have been the more natural and kindly thing to do.

Mark 10:46. Jesus gave Bartimaeus the same treatment as he did the other blind men. If Bartimaeus had not been persistent and aggressive, willing to do anything to stop Jesus and to get near to him, the Lord apparently would have left him there, sitting in the dust, blind and begging.

Luke 4:24-27. Thousands perished in the famine and from leprosy; yet God ignored them all except for the few. Why? Jesus made no attempt to explain the mysteries of divine providence; he simply stated the fact. Yet some who found a place of faith in God were rewarded with a miracle. The same option is available to us.

Luke 24:28. If the two disciples had not pressed Jesus to stay with them, he would presumably have gone on his way, and they might never have found another opportunity to experience such a stunning self-revelation of their risen Lord.

John 5:1-5. So many pitiful invalids; yet Jesus gave attention only to one of them! Yet others surely could have arrested his attention, and gained a miracle from him, if they had only had a heart to call upon him vigorously!

Mark 6:48. How incredible the saying is: "He intended to pass by them!" He was going to leave them there, perhaps to drown, and apparently would have done so if they had not halted him by their cries! If you doubt that, look around you. Every day the Master "passes by" people in desperate need, without making any attempt to help them, unless they compel his attention by faith!

I cannot tell you why Christ was (and is) seemingly so indifferent to the pain and peril of all those people. But I do know that his apparent callous disregard of their need could be changed. Those who had the courage, the passion, the faith, to demand that he take notice of them, and work the miracle they needed, were heard!

That principle of faith has not changed. It will work for you as it did for them. You have a right to meet Christ as the Great Physician. Healing belongs to you now! It is your possession! Even if the Lord has delayed hastening to your sick bed; even if he appears deaf to your cry; do not surrender your right. Faith, bold faith, determined faith, faith that refuses to be silent, can finally cause him to say to you as he did to them, "What do you want me to do for you?" and, "According to your faith be it done to you!"

Are there any conditions attached to the healing covenant? Yes there are. Some of those conditions can be found in the scriptures given above. Others can be found in the following: Exodus 15:26; Deuteronomy 7:12-17; 28:58-61; James 5:13-16; Psalm 66:16-20 (especially verse 18); etc. How closely do those conditions have to be met? You would mistaken if you supposed that they must be kept to the letter, or healing will be denied. We should try to meet the conditions as nearly as possible; but for the remainder we must trust the mercy of God and not allow a deceitfully nagging conscience to cheat us out of God's blessing (compare Psalm 103:13-14, 11-12, 1- 5).

But what if you seem to have fulfilled all reasonable requirements, yet still your prayer for healing is not heard? Why does the Lord continue to ignore a request that should be granted?

There are many mysteries in life and in the providence of God. Unless the reason for an apparent denial of our prayer, or for a delay, can be readily found, it is better not to ask "why?"; rather, you should just keep on firmly gripping the promise until the answer does come. If death intervenes before healing is found, then the fulfillment of the promise must be located in the resurrection.[1]

Meanwhile, here are some things that may prevent a perfect outworking of the healing covenant: our personal faith is rarely as strong as it should be; Satan seems stronger sometimes than he is at others; community unbelief can hinder the power of God (Mark 6:5-6); division in the church can weaken the benefits of the cross even for those who are in good fellowship (1 Corinthians 11:29-30); and so on.

An individual can do little to overcome such influences except cling to the covenant and cry out to the Lord boldly - as those people did in the gospels, when they overcame the reluctance of Christ to give them the miracle they wanted.

The problem, of course, is not a new one. Many Psalms express the poet's complaints about God, who often seemed to be distant, uncaring, and reluctant to fulfil his promises. God's response was simply to demand tougher faith

---

[1] See my book *Discovery* for an extensive discussion on this problem.

(compare Jeremiah 15:18-21; and again, notice Jeremiah's complaint in 12:1-4, and God's hard response in verse 5. There are many similar examples in the Psalms and prophets.)[2]

If you are struggling with the pain of unanswered prayer, take courage again from the example of the two blind men (Matthew 20:32). Suppose some disease other than blindness had afflicted them, or they had needed some miracle other than healing, would Jesus have asked the same question. Would his response to their faith have been the same?

Surely, if those blind men had come to Christ with any other problem or need that lay within the scope of his covenant, his response would have been the same. Seeing such passionate faith, such bold importunity, such unquenchable determination, he would still have said, "What do you want me to do for you?" *And if they had said with the same pungency, "Lord, loose us from sin," or "Lord, meet our financial need," or "Lord, heal my daughter," and so on, his reply would still have been:* "According to your faith let it be done for you!" *(Matthew 9:29).*

The important thing to note in this story, and others like it, is not that these were blind men whose sight Jesus restored, but that they were people who gained a miracle from an apparently reluctant Christ by the dogged and demanding persistence of their faith. The same kind of persistence can bring you the miracle you need.

CONCLUSION

There are many other things that the Father has already provided for you in Christ: you have a right to possess peace, and his presence, and power, and so on. The rest of this book will talk about many of them. But in the meantime, don't let the thief rob you! **Possess your possessions!!**

---

[2] The case of Jeremiah is looked at below, in chapter three, "When the promise Fails."

POINTS TO PONDER

(1) How did Israel fail to possess its possessions?

(2) How does failure to "possess your right to pardon" destroy your hope of obtaining any other great answer to prayer?

(3) What gives you the right to say, "Search can be made for my sins, but none will be found!"?

(4) Find places where the Bible says that God is willing to give us money in answer to prayer. Are there any conditions attached to those promises?

(5) Define the meaning of Ephesians 1:3.

(6) What causes people to be timid about asking God for money? How can that timidity be overcome?

(7) Why does Christ sometimes seem reluctant to heal? Why is healing sometimes delayed? Is there any value in even asking such questions?

(8) Are there any conditions attached to the healing covenant? If so, what are they?

(9) Think about Matthew 20:32. Suppose they had had some problem other than blindness, or some need other than healing, would Jesus have asked the same question. Would his response to their faith have been the same?

(10) Which of your possessions have you failed to possess? How should you now set about possessing your possessions?

HOW TO PLEASE GOD!

> *"Without faith it is impossible to please God, for when you come to God you must believe that he is, and that he is the Rewarder of those who diligently seek him."* (Hebrews 11:6).

It is difficult to convey in English how strong that declaration is in Greek, but let me attempt a paraphrase: "You will be quite unable to bring God any pleasure, no matter what you do, or how or when you do it, unless you have faith!"

The demand for faith is unavoidable. Faith has no substitute. There is nothing you can offer in its place and still hope to please God. If you want bold access to heaven's throne, you had better come with faith! "Would you come to God?" said the apostle, "Then you MUST believe!"

He uses a powerful imperative - you *must* believe, you simply and absolutely *must*! The Greek word is *dei*, which is more emphatic even than the English "must". Among the pagans, *dei* was associated with the irresistible power of Fate, that mysterious force before which all gods and men had to yield. Not even mighty Zeus, the Lord of Olympus, could escape the decrees of Fate.

Herodotus illustrates the force of *dei* in his story of the fabulously wealthy Croesus, the king of Lydia. Croesus was hungry to expand his dominion, so he decided to attack Persia. But first he craved a favorable word from heaven. So he sent an array of magnificent gifts to the oracle at Delphi in the hope of buying the support of the gods. The Pythonness told him that if he attacked Persia he would *"destroy a great empire"*. Much encouraged he went to war, and was mauled by the Persians. He had failed to ask *which* empire would fall!

Croesus sent his chains and a bitter message to the oracle, complaining that he had been deceived. The Pythonness replied that not even the highest of the gods could escape the destiny ordained for all living things. Every person's fate is predetermined, and no gift or sacrifice can alter what is decreed.[3]

The Greeks had another story, which told how the goddess of Fate wove a linen thread of measured length for each new-born soul. Every day, the goddess paid out the thread, little by little, until she reached the mark. At that moment it was

---

[3] Herodotus, The Histories I.90-92.

cut from the spindle, and the soul was doomed to die. Nothing could prolong its life on earth. This was *dei*, the unalterable decree, an imperative that cannot be denied nor avoided.

The ancient Greeks therefore associated *dei* with anything that was seen to be a fixed necessity. It described the irresistible purpose of heaven; it was applied to any predetermined fate; it represented invincible authority, and whatever was unshakeable in force or will.

The early Christians took hold of *dei*, separated it from its pagan roots, and added to it the special meaning of "a Divine necessity" - that is, something decreed by the immutable, indestructible, unalterable will of God. John used it that way: *"The revelation of Jesus Christ, which God gave him to show his servants what <u>must</u>* (dei) *soon take place"* (Revelation 1:1).

Nothing in heaven, on earth, or in hell can prevent what God has spoken from happening! Indeed, whatever God has spoken with the force of *dei* is as binding upon *him* as it is upon *us*, because it stems from his own decree, which cannot lie. That is why we can have such unshakeable confidence in his promise (Hebrews 6:17-19).

So that is the word found in our text: *"You <u>must</u> believe!"*

The sense is: "Before you even begin to draw near to God, you must, you simply <u>must</u> get your faith into good order." Unless you do, there is no hope of pleasing God!

But what does "get your faith into good order" mean? The apostle declares that faith must begin by believing three things -

FAITH KNOWS THAT GOD "EXISTS"

The original text is forthright. It reads literally, *"Believe that God is!"* Not merely that he has existence, but that he is truly present in your now, at the very heart of your situation, at the centre of your circumstances. Your God is not far distant, but closer to you than your own flesh -

> **Speak to Him thou, for he hears,**
> **And spirit with Spirit can meet -**
> **Closer is He than breathing,**
> **And nearer than hands and feet!**

God is!

What is he? He is now! He is real! He is near at hand! He is attentive to your prayer! He is able! He is concerned about you! He is interested in your welfare! He is merciful and kind! He is Saviour and Healer! He is not tomorrow but today! He is the same yesterday, today, and forever! He is willing to answer your prayer, and to bring you your heart's desires!

On one occasion the Lord God rebuked Israel because the people thought he was restricted to only one place; they did not realize he was everywhere -

> *"Can anyone hide in secret places so that I cannot see him?" declares the Lord heaven and earth?" declares the Lord!" (Jeremiah 23:23-24)*

Jeremiah demands that we live with an awareness of God's presence. Indeed, real faith, miracle-working faith, is hardly possible without such an awareness. But any believer who does have a deep sense of God's nearness, will find it hardly possible to pray without faith!

We have been taught to walk "by faith, not by sight" - that is, not to need nor to depend upon any experience of God's presence. There is, of course, much truth in that teaching. Sometimes God himself tests our faith by withdrawing from us (or at least by seeming to withdraw). But to live constantly without any feeling of God, and to be content with such a state, is a failure of faith, not a triumph.

True faith will continue to believe, whether or not God seems to be near; but true faith will also strive vigorously to regain an awareness of God. It is never satisfied with perpetual loneliness. It hungers to hold God's hand. It yearns to see, or at least to sense, the beauty of the Lord.

How fervently godly people of old pleaded with the Lord to restore his presence to them! What anguish gripped their souls when it seemed that their God had forsaken them! How bitterly and urgently they cried out for him to clothe them again with his glory! (See Psalm 27:4-5; and notice, in vs., 6, how the psalmist reckoned that victory would be his after he had met with God. See also Psalm 22:1; 51:9-11; 139:7-10 etc.).

Is it merely a coincidence that our text (He 11:6) follows hard upon the story of one of the great God-pleasers of scripture? His name was Enoch, the man who walked with God (vs. 5). So close was his fellowship with the Father, and so great was his resulting faith, that he escaped death and was raptured into heaven.

What else can we conclude, except that a close walk and mighty faith are inseparable?

Thus irresistible faith begins here: it believes that God is; it comes into the presence of God; it steps right up to the throne; it speaks to God, not from far away, but near to his face!

FAITH KNOWS THAT GOD "REWARDS"

> *"If you come to God, you must believe that he is, and that he is the REWARDER of those who diligently seek him."*

The apostle uses another arresting expression: *"Rewarder"*. The original word, in the Greek text, is unique. Prior to this occurrence scholars have not been able to find it in any other ancient Greek writing. So it seems to have been coined by the apostle himself.

Perhaps he was striving to express a wonderful idea about God, but could not find an existing word to satisfy his thought, so he invented a new one. He put together three words to form a compound noun that means literally, *"he who pays back a generous wage."* It has the sense of *"one who gives richly"*; or, *"one who rewards bountifully."*

Notice that the word is a proper noun, not a verb (as it is sometimes wrongly translated). He did not say merely that God "rewards" those who seek him, but that God's actual name is *"Rewarder"*.

If the word had been an adjective (*"the rewarding God"*), or even a verb (*"the God who rewards"*), it would have said something only about what God *does*, and that perhaps only seldom. But as a proper noun it describes what God *is*, his inner character. This is a permanent, immutable part of his very nature. He has always been, he will always be, *The Lord, The Rewarder*.

So the apostle has given us a new name for God. We already call him *Father, Saviour, Healer, Redeemer* - now we may also call him *REWARDER!*

Further, the apostle links this name with a verbal structure that conveys the idea of continuity. It is a double re-enforcing of the idea that we must believe that God's whole disposition is toward giving bountiful answers to his people's prayers. That is, God is not just an *occasional* Rewarder; rather, it is his *habit* to reward those who seek him. He continually proves himself to be the Rewarder. He is always showing himself in that character. He can never be any other.

Faith perceives this. Faith rejoices in it. Faith depends upon it. Faith never doubts that there is a vast generosity in God.

Faith expects its rich wages - the bounty of the Lord given magnificently in answer to believing prayer!

Unhappily, most people have a problem with that concept - either because they have a poor opinion of themselves, or a poor opinion of God, or both ....

They have a poor opinion of themselves

There are times, of course, when it is proper for us to be downcast because of our sins, and to approach God contritely, even with tears. It is equally certain that we dare not remain in that state. Scripture commands us to trust the promise (1 John 1:9), to know that all sin is forgiven, and then to come boldly to the throne of grace (Hebrews 4:16). Nothing in scripture requires a believer to remain in a state of breast-beating despair. To do so is to insult the mercy of God and to despise his promise.

There is a marvelous saying of Paul's: "God has blessed us in the heavenlies with every spiritual blessing in Christ" (Ephesians 1:3).

Our word "eulogy" comes from the Greek word translated "blessed" in that passage. Both words have the same basic meaning: "to speak well of someone".

Up there, in the heavenlies, what is God saying about you? Is he denouncing you, calling you a miserable worm, worthless flotsam, vile sewage? Is he angrily planning how he can punish you? Does he watch for every opportunity to do you some mischief? Is he impatiently waiting for you to pray, only so that he can spitefully refuse to bless you?

Some people, perhaps unconsciously, expect such an attitude from God, because that is how they think about themselves. That is what they feel they deserve. But if you have truly repented of your sins, and have trusted in the blood of the everlasting covenant, then you have a right to think as well of yourself as God thinks of you.

Paul is emphatic. He says that God is speaking well of you in heaven. But now you must respond by speaking well of yourself on earth. Your opinion on this matter, as on every matter, must echo the opinion of God. To do otherwise is to make God a liar - which is hardly the way to please him!

Because God has a high opinion of you in Christ, every spiritual blessing is properly yours - that is, you have a right to claim the fulfillment of every promise that belongs to you. But you will never be bold enough to lodge that claim so long as you keep on speaking poorly about one whom God has "eulogized"!

Learn then to say about yourself what God says. Because you have come into union with Christ through faith, the Father speaks well of you, and he desires to enrich you with every blessing contained in his wide promise.

They have a poor opinion of God

Honestly, what name do you give God in your deepest spirit? Do you echo the excited cry of the apostle: *"I call him my REWARDER"*? Or would you more truthfully call him *"Niggard"* - an ancient title for a stingy and close-fisted miser?

Or there is another term that aptly describes the opinion some people have about God. If they dared, they would call him *"Skinflint"* - a piece of thieve's slang for a person so mean that he would try to skin a flint just to save a few pennies!

Is that how you feel about the Father? Or do you truly expect him to overflow with generosity and kindness, rewarding you bountifully when you seek him? If you would *"please"* the Father, you had better call him *Rewarder* and expect good things from him!

We have now seen the first two parts of the kind of faith that pleases God. But there is a third thing we must believe -

FAITH KNOWS THAT GOD "DELAYS"

You may be protesting, "But I *have been* asking God for golden blessings, yet I have not received even a handful of dust!"

That is a perplexing problem. It is probably impossible, if you commit yourself to pray great prayers and to expect great things, not to experience the frustration of seeming to be ignored by an indifferent heaven. I do not have all the answers to that problem; but our text does provide one important clue (Hebrews 11:6) -

> *"Anyone who comes to God must believe that he is the Rewarder of those who seek him <u>diligently</u>."*

Note, God rewards, not those who merely seek him, but those who *diligently* seek him. Once again, in a passage full of strong words, this word is also strong. The Greek verb is an intensified form of an ordinary expression meaning "look for" or "ask for" - as though the apostle had written it in italics and then underlined it, like this: *"seek God **<u>diligently</u>**!"*

This "diligence" in prayer demands two things-

<u>Persistence</u>

Some preachers have suggested that if you pray for something more than once, then every prayer except the last must have been unbelieving. I can find no support in scripture for arguing that faith will be content to pray only once, and no more.

On the contrary, Jesus himself linked faith with persistent prayer, in the parable told in Luke 18:1-8.

He taught the same idea in his famous saying about *"asking, seeking, and knocking"* (Luke 11:9-10). There is a rising intensity in the three verbs, moving from *ask*, to *seek*, to *knock*. And by his use of the present continuous tense, Jesus demands constant, persistent prayer. He said literally, *"ask, and keep on asking; seek, and keep on seeking; knock, and keep on knocking."* The sense of the passage is simply, if your prayer is not granted when you ask, then begin to seek; and if it is not answered when you seek, then begin to knock; and if it is still not answered after you knock, then *keep on doing all three until it is answered!*

The reason lies in the mystery of God's providence: sometimes the Father chooses to delay the answers we so earnestly desire. We may or may not discover the reasons for that delay. In any case, faith will continue in prayer, refusing to allow any tardiness, whether short or long, to undermine its confident boast that God is the Rewarder of those who persistently seek him. After all, if prayer were always answered instantly, there would be no point in promising a special reward to the diligent!

Patience

Faith hardly ever stands alone. Almost always in scripture it is associated with other words. One of them (as we have just seen) is "persistence", and another is "patience" - see Hebrews 10:35-39; 6:12.

If the promise delays - and there will certainly be times when it *will* delay - then wait for it! Do not act hastily, as Abraham did, and produce an "Ishmael" to be a constant embarrassment and pain to you. There is only one way to walk with God, and that is to walk *with* him. If you run ahead you will run alone. If you scamper off impatiently to this side or that, you will be isolated away from his help.

You may never know why God chooses to delay the answer to this prayer or that, or why his promise sometimes seems so sluggish in fulfillment, but you can be sure that such delays are a normal part of the life of faith. Through them the Lord is working out his good purpose. If you continue to call the Lord your Shepherd, whether he is leading you through green pastures or through the shadowed valley of death, you will eventually discover, as did the psalmist, all the riches of his goodness and mercy.

Faith truly brings a great reward. Especially to those "who believe that God exists, and that he is the Rewarder of those who diligently seek him!"

POINTS TO PONDER

(1) What Greek word did the apostle use when he said, "You must believe," and what was its meaning in the ancient world?

(2) What special meaning did the early Christians give to that word?

(3) Think about what it means to "believe that God <u>is</u>."

(4) Who was the first man in the Bible to "please" God, and how did he do it?

(5) What does it mean to say that the Greek word for "rewarder" is a proper noun?

(6) Is there anything in the Greek text to show whether that divine title was temporary or permanent?

(7) What is God's opinion of you as a believer in Christ?

(8) What quality must be added to believing prayer to make it pleasing to God?

(9) Think about what it means to pray "persistently".

(10) Think about what it means to pray "patiently".

GOD'S MIGHTY PROMISES

> "May you always enjoy abundant grace and peace, through knowledge of God and of our Lord Jesus. His divine power has given us everything we need for life and godliness, through our knowledge of him who called us to his own glory and excellence. That is why he has given us his very great and very precious promises, for by them you can escape the corruption that has infected the world with lust, and may begin to share the very nature of God." (2 Peter 1:2-4)

What an incredible array of promises! Even more amazing than the promises is Peter's assumption that he is describing, not some kind of super-saint, but an ordinary every-day Christian. Nothing in his words suggests that he was writing to a special group of people or that he was saying anything unusual. Peter addressed his letter to ordinary Christians, and he apparently assumes that what he is saying is applicable to normal Christian life. Yet he describes a life of excellence, of glory, of grace and power, of victory, and of abundance! Amazing as it might seem, that is God's program for you.

Why then do so few people match this cheerful picture of a normal Christian life? Because there is a key: at the heart of each of the three verses of our text Peter places the word of God; that is, there is no other way by which we can possess "all things", including the Father's own "life, godliness, glory, excellence, deliverance, and divine nature," except by "his very great and very precious promises"!

Now that means that the secret of a wonderful life in Christ lies in establishing a proper relationship with the word of God. The fullness of the astonishing salvation God has made available to us in Christ cannot be realized in you and me until we become united with scripture.

Why should scripture be so important? Because the Bible is not just another piece of religious writing. It is "in-breathed" by the Holy Spirit (2 Timothy 3:16); God himself is present in scripture, revealing himself to the heart of love and to the eye of faith. We encounter God in scripture and we cannot know him apart from scripture. It is therefore imperative to meet him regularly through the open pages of the Bible. To be weak in scripture is to be weak; to be strong in scripture is to be strong.

No Christian can ever dispense with Bible reading. Scripture is more necessary to the real health of our souls than regular meals are to the health of our bodies (Job 23:12, "I have treasured the words of his mouth more than my daily bread.") *You should diligently read your Bible, the hard parts as well as the easy ones, as a matter of discipline and balanced spiritual diet. Christ can be found in every book (Luke 24:27). The voice of God may speak to the readers' heart from any page (Proverbs 6:22-23).*

This means that we must

COME TO THE WORD

All connection with scripture must surely begin here: an open Bible, and someone reading it. How can the word of God get any entrance into your life unless you actually come to your Bible day by day, open it, read it, meditate upon it, and get it off the printed page and into your head. Yet surveys show that fewer than 25% of Christians have read the whole Bible even once. The percentage who have read every part of it many times is infinitesimal! No wonder the church is weak. No wonder the saints fall defeated. No wonder the devil laughs at the average believer. Make no mistake: if you lack the word you will lack everything. But to be rich in the word is to be rich in everything!

So, if you have not already done so, you should at once develop a program that will take you right through your Bible over and over again. There is simply no substitute for coming to the word of God, regularly, consistently, as the first step toward a life of joyous victory.

However, do be on your guard against allowing that wily foe Satan to trap you into turning Bible reading into a "good work". He will do this by pulling you away from grace into law, so that reading your Bible becomes a matter of righteousness. The test is simple: do you feel that God is on your side when you stick to your program, but against you if you don't? After you have read the Bible, do you feel that you have more right than you had before to approach the throne of God in prayer? Are you depending upon your Bible reading to give you better access to God, or a stronger claim upon his favor?

If your answer is "yes" then you have allowed the devil to entice you into legalism. Instead of bringing you life, your Bible reading will now become a source of spiritual death. Understand this: you are no better in God's sight, nor any more deserving of his love, merely because you have read the Bible; nor will you be any worse, nor any less deserving of his love, if you fail to read it. Bible reading is not a way to bribe God into doing more for you than he would have done before. Our only claim upon God, and our only access to his throne, must be found in Jesus and in the total righteousness he imparts to us by pure grace.

But if not to purchase a right to heaven's blessing, why then should you read your Bible each day? Simply to receive life. For example: are you morally any better or any worse if you eat or don't eat breakfast? Of course not. But you might find yourself deficient in vitality. And if you are too negligent about your meals you will eventually ruin your health. So too with scripture. It is bread for our souls. Spiritual energy, liveliness of faith, toughness and resilience in dealing with the kingdom of darkness, all depend upon a balanced and regular diet of the word of God!

But I must warn you again about the fearful trap of legalism. We are all often guilty of turning a means of grace into an act of self-made righteousness; or of turning a gift of God into a personal "good work", upon which we make a claim for the Father's favor. He will have none of it (Romans 3:21-22, 27-28; 4:4-5; 5:1-2; etc.). Yet the carnal side of our nature remains hungry to build its own righteousness, refusing to be content with the totally adequate righteousness God has made freely available to us in Christ (Romans 5:17; 10:3-4). So there is always pressure on us to turn anything we do for God (whether prayer, worship, tithing, witnessing, Bible reading, or whatever) into a works-based means of persuading God to be good to us. But every such attempt is loathsome to God. Away with it all! Trust Jesus alone as your all-sufficient access to the Father's throne (Hebrews 4:14-16; 10:19-23). All other things will then find their proper place as merely the channels through which the riches of God's love flow to us on the basis of our trust in Christ alone.

Think back to those times when you put your neck into the noose of legalism. Can you recognize the resultant spiritual death that shriveled your soul? If so, you will realize why many people (perhaps including yourself) gain no joy from Bible reading, why they find no pleasure in God's word. They cannot read scripture without feeling self-righteous about their reading. So each time they read, the word strangles them instead of liberating them. No wonder they weary of it!

Ask yourself: do you feel more righteous if you read your Bible, and less righteous if you don't? You are under law, not grace. Do you feel that God will bless your day if you begin with Bible reading, but the devil will curse your day if you don't? You are under law, not grace. By all means establish a regular program of Bible reading; but sternly prevent your flesh from turning it into a ritual law by which you expect to obtain the favor of God. Stand fast rather in the liberty wherewith Christ has set you free and absolutely refuse to be entangled again in a yoke of legal bondage (Galatians 5:1).

CONCEIVE THE WORD

I know a person who has not only read the Bible right through countless times, but he has memorized it from cover to cover, not just in English, but many versions in many languages! He can quote instantly from any part of them all with equal ease. Yet he remains the most wretched person you could ever meet - craven, anxious, deceitful, wracked with miseries. He has certainly "come" to the Bible, but his astonishing knowledge of it brings him no benefit. Indeed, every word of scripture is like the blow of a scourge upon his back. Who is he? You know him as well as I - his name is Satan! (Note James 2:19b.)

The devil's problem is this: he can memorize scripture well enough, and has done so in every language on earth; but he can never get a revelation *of the word. Therefore its real energy, its powerful promise, always eludes him. What the believing Christian experiences when the scripture becomes alive in his or her heart remains an unfathomable mystery to Satan.*

Thus Satan is a clear example of the principle that you can come to the word of God, yet remain defeated and dispirited unless you go on to conceive the word. Before the promises of God can become effective in your life, they must make an 18-inch journey - from your head down into your heart.

To "conceive" the word means to get an inner revelation of the word, to get it out of your mind and into your spirit, to have your "spiritual eyes" opened, to "know" deeply, personally, vitally, the gospel riches and power that are available in Christ to the Spirit-filled believer.

We all experience a kind of "credibility gap" when we read the promises of God. The promise seems so ephemeral; our need seems so substantial. We sense a hiatus between where we are and where the promise is. That chasm must be bridged. The promise must catch fire in our hearts, blazing into light and truth, so that now the promise is the only thing that is true and all else is a lie!

Prayer is the main path to that transformation, as Paul shows by his own prayers (and see also Elisha's prayer in the delightful story in 2 Kings 6:15- 17.) Satan is well able to memorize *scripture, but* revelation *in it is impossible for him, for God reveals his word only to those who have the right kind of eyes and ears and heart (1 Corinthians 2:9-16).*

Answer this question: what was the main burden of Paul's prayers for the churches he founded? He did not pray that God would give them a mighty revival, nor that the Father would pour out his Spirit upon them, nor that great miracles would happen, nor that their financial needs would be met, and the like. In fact, he did not ask God to give those churches any of the things that are the constant burden of our prayer meetings. I don't mean that it is wrong to pray for such things. But Paul had a better understanding. And what was that? You will find the answer in his prayers in Ephesians 1:16-23; Colossians 1:9-14. He asked for one thing only: that God would give the churches a revelation in his word.

Compare that with prayer meetings you have been to. When were you last in a meeting where the main focus of prayer was the same as Paul's? Could this be why so many of our prayer meetings are ineffectual? Are we endlessly praying for the wrong thing?

Make Paul's prayers your own. Give heaven no rest until the promises of God explode into a glorious reality within your spirit. Then you will truly find yourself living in the dynamic of the "immeasurable greatness of the power God accomplished in Christ when he raised him from the dead and made him sit at his own right hand in the heavenlies!"

CONFESS THE WORD

Psalm 31:19 says, "Oh! how marvelous are the rich things God has prepared for those who publicly declare that he will deliver them!"

God's exceedingly great and precious promises become effective only when they are boldly spoken in faith. In other words, you can come *to the word, and conceive the word, and yet still fail to obtain the promise unless you go on to confess the word. Having put the promise into your head, and then into your heart, you must now bring it into your mouth!*

Scores of scriptures put before us the necessity of openly and vigorously speaking out whatever promise you want fulfilled in your life. Bold confession activates the promise. Why is this so? Why does God demand that we overcome reticence, shyness, timidity, and vocalize his promise? Why does fulfillment of the promise depend upon you speaking it aloud? I cannot say. I only know that scripture is unequivocal in its demand that the word must be spoken by your mouth as well as believed in your heart.

Here is an illustration of a similar rule at work in the natural world. Think about the voice-activated switches and locks that are now available. A whole house can be equipped with them, so that every door will lock or unlock, every device will switch on or off, simply in response to a spoken command. These switches can also be programmed to respond to the sound of only one particular voice. Which I imagine would be convenient and secure, unless the owner happens to contract laryngitis! Then, no matter how much he wishes or wills for the door to open he will find himself locked out of his own house. Plenty of energy is available in the switches and locks, but only one catalyst can release that energy: the sound of the owner's voice!

So are the promises of God. They are replete with the staggering resurrection-power of Christ himself; but only one key can unlock that limitless strength: the sound of the voice of faith. *That is the catalyst that unleashes the spiritual force of the promise. In chemistry, a catalyst is a substance that activates a reaction between two or more other substances, but remains itself unchanged in the process. So in the walk of faith, your believing confession of the promise of God brings the power of the promise into contact with your need and begins the process whereby the miracle you desire is made to happen. Again, just as some chemical reactions cannot begin until the right catalyst is added, so the promise of God lies dormant in relation to your need until you arouse it by the quickening sound of faith's bold affirmation of that promise.*

How do you speak in the hour of need? Suppose you were sick. How would you speak about that sickness? How would you speak to it? (Mark 11:22-24). What would your "confession" be? Would you know how to take authority and how to command in faith? What words would you use to activate God's promise of healing?

CONTEND FOR THE WORD

Sometimes, even after you have got the word into your head (by coming to it), your heart (by conceiving it), and your mouth (by confessing it), the promise may still remain elusive and unfulfilled. How can that be? Because three strong enemies work against the realization of the promise of God in your life: the world, the flesh, the devil. Those foes often oblige us to fight the fight of faith, to stand firm, confident that what God has spoken will surely be done (1 Kings 8:56).

Psalm 31 (which I quoted above) shows this principle. Despite its eulogy of the "abundant goodness" *God has laid up for us, the psalm still warns the warrior to* "be strong, and let your heart take courage, all you who wait for the Lord" *(verse 24; see also 1 Corinthians 15:58; 16:13).*

So then, never abandon that confidence in God, which alone can bring you his great reward (Hebrews 10:35-39). Having done the will of God, endure with boldness, stand with steadfast trust, until you receive what has been promised. God finds no pleasure in those who shrink back from what he has called them to believe and to receive. Determine rather to be among that adventurous company who refuse to be dismayed, who rise up in Jesus' name and possess their possessions!

POINTS TO PONDER

(1) Do you agree that 1 Peter 1:3-4 was not written to describe an extraordinary but on the contrary an ordinary Christian life? If so, in what way does the passage convey that idea?

(2) What is the major fault that prevents most Christians from enjoying the quality of life described by Peter?

(3) Have you read the whole Bible, or only parts of it? Why is it important to read all of it? Could a point be reached in Christian life where it would no longer be necessary to read the Bible regularly? If not, why not?

(4) Think of some ways in which you could plan to read your Bible right through, over and over again.

(5) If someone establishes a regular programme of Bible reading, what is one great peril he or she will need to guard against? Have you ever fallen into that trap?

(6) How do people turn a gift that God gave them as a source of life into a Satanic tool of death? How do they turn grace into law, the "Spirit that gives life" into a "letter that kills"?

(7) What does it mean to "conceive" the word of God? How can that be achieved? Why is it impossible for Satan to do so?

(8) What was Paul's main burden in prayer for the churches he had founded?

(9) In a time of sickness, or of some other need, whether physical, material, or spiritual, how would you "confess" the word of God?

(10) What is the significance of the "sound" of the voice of faith?

HOW TO BE MADE WHOLE!

How important is faith? Can the way you believe really change what God does for you?

Luke gives a strong answer to those questions. He tells the incredible story of ten lepers who were instantly healed by Jesus (17:11-19). Among them was one who exceeded his colleagues. He gained from the Master an additional and even more extraordinary miracle.

Like his friends, initially he was only "healed" of his leprosy (verse 15; the Greek word means simply "to cure a disease") - but now he is "made whole". Every trace of leprosy has vanished! His wasted limbs and maimed extremities are restored, the scars and blemishes left by the disease have disappeared!

That was amazing enough. Yet here is an even more arresting fact: Jesus did not attribute this extraordinary miracle to his own power, but to the strength of the leper's faith!

What would you have expected Jesus to say to the leper? Surely something like this: "Stand up and go your way, for by my own miracle-working authority I have made you whole!" Instead, he said to the leper: "<u>Your faith</u> has made you whole!" (verse 19).

At once we are prevented from falling into two common errors:

- ♦ the fault of thrusting such miracles into the past, as though they require the physical presence of Jesus, yet time and space cannot limit faith; and

- ♦ the fault of making them dependent upon some arbitrary act of God.

The leper gained a miracle, not because he was fortunate enough to be alive during a special dispensation of healing, nor because God selected him alone to receive a miracle, but because he chose to believe the promise of God and to seize the opportunity Jesus offered him. *The strength of his own faith alone was sufficient to change dramatically the outcome of his personal encounter with Christ!*

Now if that man could believe and be made whole, then we are compelled to allow the possibility of us doing the same. The laws of faith remain true in every generation.

What are those laws? What are the ingredients of the kind of faith that can bring you good health and victory over all the works of darkness?

GREAT FAITH SEES CHRIST AS SAVIOR AND HEALER

The irresistible pressure of the leper's faith, compelled Jesus to respond to him in a special way. The expression the Master used ("Your faith has made you whole!") has more significance than you may think. *It was a kind of standard formula, often employed by Christ to convey to people both healing and pardon. Apart from our text, Luke records this same formula also in 8:48 (when Jesus healed a woman's hemorrhage), and in 18:42 (when Jesus healed a blind man). In each of those places, Christ spoke exactly the same words. In the Greek text, not even one syllable is different.*

But even more striking is Jesus' use of the same expression when he spoke to a harlot (7:50). The English version reads, "Your faith has saved you!" *Yet the Greek text is identical to the other places:* "Your faith has made you whole!"

Clearly, faith that brings pardon of sin, may also bring healing of sickness.

Saviour and Healer

Christ is Saviour and Healer, and both of those attributes are reached by faith. If it is still valid to say to a sinner, "Your faith in Christ can make you spiritually whole," then it is equally valid to say to a sick person, "Your faith in Christ can make you physically whole!" Jesus allows no distinction between those two benefits. He wants people to be whole: spiritually and physically. Both remedies come in response to faith.

Why is this? Simply because Christ came to make you whole, not just your soul, nor your body, but your entire being (1 Thessalonians 5:23-24; 3 John 2; etc.). In the reckoning of Luke (and of all the apostles), salvation includes healing, and healing includes salvation. Ideally, both benefits should always go hand in hand; there should be no distinction between them.

Therefore, in response to faith, Christ is equally willing to show himself as Saviour or Healer, and preferably both. In New Testament terms, to deny one is also to deny the other, for scripture uses the same word of both: Christ is the One who makes you whole.

A Peculiar Contrast

Now here is a peculiar contrast. The Jews accepted the healing miracles of Christ, but were deeply angered when he offered pardon for sin (Luke 7:50; and compare 5:20-26). They were not much troubled when he said to a sick *person, "Your faith has made you whole"; but let him say the same to a* sinful *person and their fury was boundless!*

We face an opposite problem. No one today is offended when we say to sinners, in Jesus' name, "Your faith has brought you pardon." But let us claim that faith can also heal them physically, and we are at once damned as heretics!

Yet if we admit that Christ has power to pardon, but doubt his willingness to heal, are we any better than they who accepted his power to heal, but questioned his right to pardon? Both faults place a barrier around the divine prerogative. Both faults sunder the unity of human nature. Mark it again: the Father is not more concerned about either your body or your soul. He is concerned about you. *He wants* you - *your whole being - to be sound and well in every way.*

A Challenge to Faith

Christ challenged the Jewish leaders to acknowledge that his healing miracles proved he has power to forgive sins. Now he challenges us to believe the reverse: if he has power to pardon, then he certainly has power to heal!

But both depend upon faith. You will be saved if you believe. You will be healed if you believe. Nor is there any difference in the required faith. The faith that makes us whole spiritually is identical with the faith needed to make us whole physically. If you can believe in Christ as Saviour, you should equally well believe in him as Healer. The one should be no more difficult than the other.

A Painful Problem

This raises a problem: why is healing so often much more difficult to obtain than pardon? No doubt there are many reasons, and they vary from person to person. But you could note the following:

- ♦ often the reverse is true, for there are still many people, like the Jews of old, who find it easier to accept that Jesus can heal them than that he can pardon them. Even deeply committed Christians are sometimes driven to doubt their salvation, and have to struggle fiercely in faith to recapture their sense of the peace and presence of God. In other words, it may not be so easy to embrace salvation as we are carelessly prone to think (John Bunyan, for example, graphically describes the faith-struggles of a true Christian in Pilgrim's Progress.)

- Jesus himself acknowledged that it really is more difficult to say, "Stand up and walk," than to say, "Your sins are forgiven" (Luke 5:23-25). The reason is obvious. There is no way of telling for sure (apart from just trusting God) whether a sinner has been pardoned; but every onlooker can tell instantly if a cripple has been made whole!

So we do have the barrier of our sense perception to overcome when we try to speak a word of healing. For all of us, at least occasionally if not usually, that is a hard barrier to break through. When it comes to pardon, we can for the present just rely on God's promise, with or without any tangible evidence. But when it comes to healing, either you are cured or you are not! The evidence one way or the other is undeniable.

Reach for the Ideal

In practice, therefore, we may find it more difficult to muster healing-faith than saving-faith; but in terms of spiritual quality there is no difference between them. If you know how to receive pardon from Christ, then ideally it should be no more difficult to receive healing, and vice versa.

Jesus himself, as a man, managed to overcome every barrier, so that for him it became as easy to act on the promise of healing as on the promise of pardon. That is the goal toward which we should all be advancing.

GREAT FAITH RESPONDS TO THE PROMISE OF GOD

The ministry of Jesus produced in Israel an awakening to the covenant promises of God. Those promises (which included physical healing, and numerous other blessings, Deuteronomy 28:1-14; 7:12-15; Psalm 103:1-5; etc.), had lain dormant for centuries. Until they met Jesus, very few of the people had had any confidence in them, nor any faith to possess them.

Christ showed that the promise still had its ancient power. Despite the passage of more than a thousand years since it was first spoken, the promise could still bring healing to anyone who believed. The leper was "made whole" because he boldly responded to Jesus' call to come back to the Word of God.

Many Promises

The same demand confronts us. If you are unsure how willing the Father is to do great things for his children, cast your eye over the following promises of answered prayer: Matthew 6:6; 7:7-11; 18:19-20; 21:21- 22; Mark 11:24-25; John 14:13-14; 15:7 & 16; 16:23-24; Romans 10:12-13; Hebrews 4:16; 1 John 3:22; 5:14; and the greatest of all, Ephesians 3:20.

Those are just a selection of promises from the New Testament alone. A full list from the whole Bible would fill this page! But even that selection shows how much we need an enlargement of faith. Scripture presents an incredible scope for prayer. The boundaries are almost limitless!

Those promises are as true today as they were when God first spoke them. But the question is: do you believe them? Do you allow them to build into your prayer an unwavering assurance? Do you expect answers from God that are as great as his promise?

Martin Luther made this pungent comment on our sluggish faith -

> "(God) desires nothing more earnestly of us than that we ask many and great things of him, and he is angry if we do not pray and petition with confidence.
>
> "If the richest and most powerful emperor were to bid a poor beggar ask for whatever he might desire and were ready to give great, princely presents, but the fool were to beg only for a serving of common soup, he would be justly considered a rogue and a scoundrel who made the command of his Imperial Majesty the object of mockery and derision, and would not be worthy to come into his presence.
>
> "In like manner, it is a disgrace and dishonor to God if we, to whom he offers and promises so many unspeakable blessings, despise them and are not confident that we shall receive them, and if we scarcely venture to ask for a morsel of bread."

Moribund Faith

Did the lack of healing miracles in Israel just prior to the ministry of Jesus prove that the promise was moribund? Of course not! The promise was still as full of life as ever it had been. Faith was ailing, not the promise!

Likewise, if healing miracles are scarce today, this is not because God has withdrawn his promise, but because the church has withdrawn its faith from the promise. Where faith is bold and eager the promise still has all its age-old power!

Faith in the Covenant

So the question is answered: on what basis did Jesus bring healing to the sick: by an act of his personal might; or by renewing their faith in the healing covenant?

There was, of course, an exercise of wonderful spiritual power in the healing ministry of Christ. Without him, there would have been no miracles (see Mark 5:30; Luke 6:19; plus many places where his miracles are attributed to Christ himself, Mark 3:7-9; John 2:23; 6:2; Acts 10:38 etc.).

Nonetheless, it is clear from the many places where Christ emphasizes the faith of the people, and from his general teaching, that Jesus saw himself as acting within the covenant God had made with Israel. He tried to focus the attention of the people on that covenant, rather than on himself.

We are in the same place. We cannot be healed apart from the action of our Great Physician; yet he insists that we come to him firmly trusting in his covenant promise. Healing, therefore, is as much due to our faith as it is to his action.

GREAT FAITH KNOWS THE POWER OF JESUS' NAME

> *"The lepers lifted up their voices and cried, `Jesus, Master, have mercy on us!'"*

Notice the important conjunction of "Jesus" and "Master". That association should never be absent from your mind. The mention of Jesus' Name should always be linked with the thought of mastery. His Name has power! It can dispel all fear; it can bring perfect wholeness, whether of spirit, soul, or body (Acts 3:16); it gives access to the heavenlies (Ephesians 1:3); it brings dominion over disease, devils, and all the power of the enemy (Mark 16:17-18; Luke 10:17- 19).

Careless Familiarity

There is no fault among Christians so prevalent as that of speaking the Name of Jesus carelessly - without any excitement, without any sense of its majestic power, without any faith that the uttering of that Name can move ponderous mountains, turning defeat into victory, disease into health, sin into righteousness, sorrow into joy, poverty into plenty.

When that Name is spoken indifferently, routinely, as a mere religious formula, faith becomes dull, and the Name (for that casual speaker) loses its efficacy.

So guard your use of that Name! Don't risk being denied access to its measureless glory! It is your most powerful spiritual weapon! (Mark 16:17-18) Don't squander this, your most magnificent resource!

Aggressive Prayer

Notice that the leper cried the Name of Jesus with a loud voice - he shouted loudly, and called out to Jesus with all his strength.

Why did he have to put so much effort into attracting Jesus' attention? Mostly because he saw that Jesus was about to leave that vicinity, and the opportunity for healing might be gone forever. That is the literal sense of verses 11-12. The Greek conveys an image of Jesus simply passing through the village, with no intention of stopping or ministering there. The inference is simply this: if the ten lepers had not captured his attention by shouting at him, Jesus would have passed them by, leaving them to perish in misery.

The gospels describe several occasions when Jesus was seemingly willing to walk past hurting people, without doing a thing to help them (Matthew 9:27; 20:30; Mark 10:46; Luke 4:24-27; 18:35 ff.; 24:28; John 5:2; and most remarkably, Mark 6:48.) Some of those people caught Jesus' attention and got a miracle from him; but many others were more quiescent, and he simply passed them by.

How inexplicable that behavior seems! Can you imagine yourself walking past, and ignoring, two blind men who were screaming for your help? Jesus went right on, and into a house, and closed the door on them. They had to stumble along behind him, and somehow push rudely into the house, before he took any notice of them (Matthew 9:27-28).

In the same way, Jesus walked right past blind Bartimaeus, and kept on walking, despite his piteous cries. Even when Jesus did stop, he compelled Bartimaeus to grope up to him, while he waited for the blind man to arrive. Surely it would have been more compassionate for Christ to walk over to where Bartimaeus was sitting? Surely Jesus should have taken the initiative in reaching out to him, and to other broken people instead of making it so hard for them to get near to him?

How is it conceivable that Christ was apparently willing to walk right past the little fleet of sinking boats on Galilee? Mark leaves no doubt, if Peter had not stopped him, the Master would have vanished into the driving storm and left the boats and their passengers to drown. Mark says: "He would have passed them by!"

I cannot explain why Christ sometimes does no more than "pass by"; but I do know that even then vigorous faith can apprehend him! If he does not intervene in your affairs on his own initiative, he certainly will on yours - if you cry out to him aggressively, insisting upon his help! (Luke 18:1-8)

GREAT FAITH RELEASES THE POWER OF PRAISE

Luke forcefully emphasizes this aspect of the leper's miracle: "he turned back, <u>praising</u> God with a <u>loud</u> voice, and he fell on his face at Jesus' feet, giving him <u>thanks</u> ... And Jesus said, 'Was no one found to give <u>praise</u> to God except this foreigner?'"

Christ spoke his healing words to the leper ("Your faith has made you whole!") in particular response to the man's exuberant praise. *Faith would have remained undiscovered without praise.*

<u>Praise And Faith</u>

Praise is the great signifier of faith. Where praise is not heard, faith does not exist.

But praise is also a stimulant of faith and is itself a vehicle of the power of God.

Real praise will sometimes be "loud" praise, forceful, alive, passionate, bold, heartfelt, joyful, and mighty in God. Indeed, since real faith is the substance of things hoped for and the assurance of things not yet seen, and since real faith already possesses the answer from God, how can it do otherwise than rejoice and be glad? (Hebrews 11:1; 1 John 5:14-15).

This will be the theme of a later chapter.

POINTS TO PONDER

(1) We might have expected Christ to say to the leper, "Stand up and go your way, for by my power I have made you whole!" But instead he said, "Your faith has made you whole!" What does that teach us about the availability of miracles today?

(2) If the terminology of the New Testament is used, is it possible to deny that Jesus is the Healer without also denying that he is the Saviour?

(3) Why do we find it more difficult to grasp healing from Christ than pardon?

(4) Is there any difference between saving-faith and healing-faith?

(5) Did the lack of healing miracles in Israel just prior to the ministry of Jesus prove that the promise was moribund? What does that say about the church in our time?

(6) On what basis did Jesus bring healing to the sick: by an act of his personal power; or by renewing their faith in the healing covenant?

(7) What do the statements in Acts 3:6,12,16 tell us about the use of the Name of Jesus?

(8) What fault most commonly enervates the Name of Jesus in the lives of Christians?

(9) Is it impious to speak the Name of Jesus aggressively, or forcefully?

(10) "Where praise is not heard, faith does not exist." Do you agree with that statement?

WHEN THE PROMISE FAILS

"O Lord, why do you tell such terrible lies? Why do you behave like a desert mirage?" (Jeremiah 15:18b)

Can a man call God a liar and live? Imagine telling God that his promises are worthless, as false as a shimmering apparition on burning sand! Even the heathen prophet Balaam had a better opinion of God: *"He is not a man that he should lie, nor a son of man, that he should change his mind!"* (Numbers 23:19).

There was a time when Jeremiah himself had held a finer confidence in the Lord, calling him, not a dried up brook, but *"the spring of living water."* In that braver hour, Jeremiah himself had sternly rebuked the people for turning away from their Sovereign (2:13).

But now the promises of God seemed to him to be no better than a mocking illusion. What changed his mind? Nothing less than the apparent failure of those same promises. What were they? You can find them in 1:9-10, 17-19. Read them, and note how incredible they are. What an authority God gave to his servant! What towering strength! What invincibility! What protection!

When he heard them, those promises overcame all Jeremiah's youthful anxieties (1:6-8); they emboldened him to seize with joy the mantle of a prophet in Israel. *"When your words came to me,"* he sang, *"I ate them; they were my joy and my heart's delight, for I bear your name, O Lord God Almighty"* (15:16). Then he went out to do God's bidding, resolutely faithful in his obedience to the word he had received (15:17).

Jeremiah kept his part of the agreement; but it seemed as though God had abandoned his. About the only part of the promise that worked, as far as the prophet could see, was the bit about *"they will fight against you!"*. All too well those words had been accomplished. Jeremiah had been beaten, imprisoned, starved, cursed, forsaken, mocked, ignored - oh! how well the entire nation had assaulted him. But the corollary promise, *"they will not overcome you,"* seemed to the hurting prophet to be a cruel mockery. He could bear it no longer. Sick, miserable, thinking himself a failure, he cried, *"Why is my pain unending and my wound grievous and incurable?"* (15:18a).

Perhaps you have had an experience like Jeremiah's? Perhaps even now you are bitter, bewildered, frustrated, full of pain, because you trusted the promise of

God, but it failed you? And now your complaint sounds in heaven, "Why did I lose my job? Why haven't you met my need? Why am I not healed? Why did you allow my child to run away? Why didn't you help me when I trusted you? Where were you God when I looked for you?"

In angry exasperation you may, like Jeremiah, finally have become bold enough to stand before God and to his very face call him a liar!

What happens to the man who accuses God of lying? I suppose that depends upon the man, and what his motives are. In Jeremiah's case, God was graciously willing to respond, and what he said to the despondent prophet is just as true for you and me, when we face the crisis of a seemingly failed promise, as it was for him.

GOD IGNORED THE PROPHET'S "WHY?"

Jeremiah was not the only person in the Bible who once felt abandoned by God. Perhaps the most perplexing example is that of Jesus, from whom the anguished cry was wrung, *"Why have you forsaken me?"* There was no answer; heaven remained silent until after the resurrection. Nor was any reply given to the psalmist who first voiced that querulous *"Why?"* (22:1-2). Job, of course, is another example. In one place he even declared -

> *"God may kill me for saying this, but I will nonetheless accuse him to his face, and defend my innocence before him!" (13:13-15, especially in several modern translations.)*

Even a casual reading of the Psalms will discover many places where the poets were perplexed by God's apparent failure to answer prayer. You will find a passionate example in Psalm 88, which is a poem of unrelenting despair, bleak in hopelessness (note verses 13, 14, & 18). Then there is Habakkuk (1:2-4, 13; 2:1), and Jeremiah again, who complained to God more than once! (See Jeremiah 12:1-2; etc.).

All of those sufferers joined with Jeremiah in lamenting, "Why are my miseries unending?" But God, when he replied to the prophet (15:19-21), completely ignored his petulant demand. The Lord refused to explain why Jeremiah's ministry had been so turbulent and fruitless, or why heaven was apparently indifferent to the violent persecution he had endured.

We too are prone to thrust at God our own "Why? Why? Why?" Sometimes nothing works out the way we thought it would, or the way we feel God has promised, and we demand an explanation from heaven. Perhaps even now you want to know why your business has failed, why your marriage is in ruins, why your child is wracked with fever, why your ungodly neighbor enjoys contented prosperity while your troubles never end? You are, of course, entitled to ask, and sometimes you might even get an answer, for there are times when God does show why things went wrong, or why something has happened to you - especially when your own sin or error is the cause of the problem (cp. 1 Corinthians 11:30; Jonah 1:7-10; etc.). There are numerous similar examples in the history of Israel; and for a slightly different problem, think about 2 Corinthians 12:7-10.

Mostly, however, the Father ignores our "Why, God, why?" We are required simply to trust his wisdom and love, never doubting that in the end all things will come together for our good (Romans 8:28).

So don't focus on the mysteries of life. Concentrate, not upon what you don't know, but upon what you do know about the Father. To persist in asking unanswerable questions is to sow frustration and rebellion, and to reap an ultimate alienation from Christ. If nothing else, you do know that your name is written down in heaven. Jesus himself warned against allowing anything less than that to affect your joy (Luke 10:19-20). Then, because your name is engraved in the Book of Life, many other great things are true: we are sons of God; we are members of his indestructible church; we have received the gift of the Holy Spirit; we have peace with God; we have an inheritance in the heavenlies; and the like.

Stop asking questions God probably will not answer. Rejoice rather in the many wonderful answers he has *given!*

GOD REPEATED HIS PROMISE

See Jeremiah 15:20-21; and compare those verses with the original promises in 1:17-19. Notice that they are nearly identical. What an extraordinary thing! Jeremiah handed God a cluster of seemingly broken promises, insisting that God do something about them, and all he got were those same promises handed right back again!

Is God callous? Was he mocking Jeremiah? Doesn't he care that we are hurting? Of course he cares. But we have to learn that in the end the Father has nothing else to give us except his promise. His word is himself. It is all his wealth and power. If his word is not good enough for you, then in the end nothing else will be good enough either.

Jeremiah had to see that finally there is no distinction between God and his word. The promise of God and the God who promised are one. Therefore, when God gives us his word he gives us himself, and there is nothing greater that he can give (cp. John 1:1; Hebrews 6:13, 17-18). Therefore to reject the word is to reject God (1 John 5:9-10). But to hold to the word is to hold to God, and therefore potentially to possess all that God is, to have access to all that he has, and to be in contact with his limitless power. Likewise, the word of faith and faith in the word are inseparable. Faith cannot exist apart from a firm grip on the word of God; but that word remains unfulfilled until it is appropriated by faith. The word both creates faith and demands faith. So God forced his word back into the prophet's spirit. He insisted that Jeremiah must abandon his complaints and simply grasp the word. The presence of God came with that word; it stirred new faith in the prophet's heart; he found courage to speak it again; he called into existence all that the word promised; he gained what his heart desired.

So you have to decide: will you or will you not believe the promise of God? Will you stand firm on that promise, or allow the world and Satan to push you off that rock and into the sinking sands of despair? Will you go forward in faith, despite every contrary force, or fall back into hopeless unbelief? The choice is yours!

If you were to turn away from prayer and come to me with your "why doesn't the promise work?" I would have the same answer for you as God had for Jeremiah: just the promise handed back to you; just the word of God. No response to your "why?"; just an admonition to hold fast to what God has spoken, confident that in God's time he will bring his promise into reality (Hebrews 10:35-39). That is all God has given me. That is all I can give you. Everything else will fail; but the promise of God is for ever! (1 Peter 1:23-25; Luke 21:33).

GOD DEMANDED A FAITH CONFESSION

See Jeremiah 15:19. Notice the importance God placed on the words Jeremiah spoke. Notice the choice the prophet had: either to keep on speaking "worthless" *words, or to begin speaking "precious" words. That is, to speak with unbelief or faith, with fear or trust, with despair or authority.*

In the walk of faith hardly anything is more important than the words you speak. You can talk yourself into or out of the miracle you need. You can speak the promise of God into or out of its fulfillment in your life. The choice is yours, and yours the responsibility for ruling your tongue.

All that God has ever done has been wrought by the spoken word. He simply speaks, and it is! Whatever he says, happens! (Hebrews 11:3; Romans 4:17b; Genesis 1:3ff.; etc.) He gave that same method to Adam and Eve, when he told them to take dominion over the earth and all that is in it. They were to rule by the spoken word (Genesis 1:26-28). Only after the Fall was man condemned to do the will of God "by the sweat of his brow" *(3:19). We have not yet escaped Adam's curse, although a portion of that lost authority has been restored to us in Christ. Thus once again, there are certain aspects of the will of God that we should accomplish simply by speaking a word of faith (cp. Mark 11:22-23; Matthew 17:20-21; 21:21-22; Luke 17:6. Notice that in each place the emphasis is not on asking God to do something, but upon you telling something to happen in the name of the Lord.)*

There have been some extreme views on this matter of a "faith confession" - as though one "negative" word would for ever destroy all hope of getting an answer to your prayer. Well, Jeremiah spoke plenty of negative words, but God did not cut him off! There is always room in prayer to be honest with God and to tell him just what is in your heart. In any case, since God already knows what is in your thoughts, and what emotions are stirring your heart, you might as well be honest with him! So tell him what you are thinking and feeling. Share everything with him: all your doubts and fears, your anger and frustration, your bewilderment and hurt.

If you are reluctant to express such things in your own words, turn to the Psalms. Probably as many as half of the Psalms are laments, containing many stanzas where the poet declares his grievance to God. The Lord can hardly be distressed if you speak his own word back to him!

Nonetheless, you cannot continue a complaint indefinitely. The moment must be reached when faith takes hold, casts bitterness aside, and raises again a song of joyful trust. So turn your words around, and resume declaring your absolute reliance upon the promise of God. Those "worthless" words of unbelief must become "precious" words of faith. Let it be sooner rather than later!

God stressed two things to Jeremiah:

- "you will become my spokesman." Let Jeremiah choose to put the "precious" words of God back into his mouth (casting aside those "worthless" words of complaint), and his mouth will then become as God's mouth. When he speaks, it will be as if God were speaking, with the same awesome results (Genesis 1:3, etc.).

Similarly, when you speak God's word, in harmony with God's will, and with unwavering faith, your voice gains the same creative power, the same irresistible authority, as if God himself were speaking! (cp. 2 Kings 1:10, 12).

- "they will turn to you, but you will not turn to them." Mark this: either the world will turn you away from God, or you will turn it toward God. There is no neutrality. One or the other will turn. You will either come under the dominion of your circumstances, or you will bring your circumstances under the dominion of faith. You and I are called in the name of Jesus to bring each situation into conformity with the word of God, so that nothing can maintain its influence over us that is antagonistic to the purpose of God (cp. Matthew 6:10).

GOD PROMISED HIM VICTORY

See Jeremiah 15:21. Nothing is so tough as spiritual authority properly exercised. If in obedience to God's command and with faith in God's promise you speak the word of God with unyielding determination, it will be done! The guarantee is unequivocal: "I will redeem you from the grasp of the cruel!"

"Spiritual authority" is the authority Christ has given us to act as his ambassadors and to impose his will upon the environment in which we live. It is authority over sin, sickness, Satan, and over everything God has told us to rule by faith (Luke 10:19; Romans 8:37; 1 John 5:4; etc.) But note, this authority does not give us immunity from persecution or distress, nor does it empower us to do anything we please, nor to possess anything we like. "Spiritual authority" is effective only when it is used to do the will of God; hence the second phrase, "properly exercised." Spiritual authority can be properly exercised only in response to a specific mandate from heaven. Faith can implement only what God wants it to implement. Any attempt to use it carnally, selfishly, or ignorantly will fail (cp. James 4:2-7). But whenever you take hold of your spiritual authority, either to fulfil the purpose of God or to demolish all that opposes his purpose in your life, then it is mighty indeed!

So it happened with Jeremiah. He took up the promise again, as he had before, and with irresistible authority brought it to fulfillment. He spoke, and vast armies marched. He spoke, and nations and kingdoms fell. He spoke, and peoples were planted and plucked, established and uprooted, built up and torn down. He spoke, and the course of history was changed. (See again 1:9-10.) He himself was delivered, as the Lord had promised, and every word he spoke in the name of the Lord came to pass. But first he had to master fear: "Do not be terrified by them, or I will terrify you before them," *was God's dread threat (1:17). And then he had to speak with dauntless faith. When he did so, not even the mightiest monarch could withstand his word. You have the same authority!*

CONCLUSION

I doubt if any of us can escape at some time confronting the same crisis that nearly ruined Jeremiah: the crisis of a failed promise. What do you do when you have claimed some beautiful promise of God only to be savagely disappointed? You could copy Job's wife, and cry, "Curse God, and die!" *(Job 1:9). You could follow Jeremiah and call God a liar. You could yield to satanic persuasion and denounce the promise of God as worthless. Or you can insist that even in the valley of the shadow of death the Lord is your Shepherd; you can trust his wisdom and goodness; you can turn back to his word; you can believe his sure promise; you can set yourself to speak that promise in the authority of faith; you can stand steadfast in joy; and you can see the mighty deliverance of the Lord!*

POINTS TO PONDER

(1) Was Jeremiah the only servant of God in the Bible to call into question God's integrity?

(2) Have you had an experience where it seemed to you that despite faith and bold confession, the promise of God failed you? What was your reaction? Were you angry with God? Or did you, like an ostrich, bury your head and refuse to face the issue?

(3) Can you think of other examples in scripture of people who asked "Why?" when life turned out wrongly for them?

(4) Does God ever tell us, when we ask "Why?"?

(5) What are some of the good things we do know about God, promises that remain sure, no matter what vicissitudes may strike us in this life?

(6) What was God's purpose in repeating his promises to Jeremiah?

(7) What does the following sentence mean? "God's word in your mouth has the same creative power, when it is spoken in faith, as it has in the mouth of God."

(8) Is it always wrong to express complaint or anger to God?

(9) "Nothing is so tough as spiritual authority properly exercised." Think about those two phrases, "spiritual authority" and "properly exercised".

(10) How literally was God's promise to Jeremiah in 1:9-10 eventually fulfilled?

POWERFUL PRAYER

Prayer is a vital key to "possessing your possessions". It is hardly possible to obtain anything from God except through the channel of answered prayer. The story of Jabez provides an example of a man who was astonishingly successful in prayer; you will find it in 1 Chronicles 4:1-10.

Did you read the whole passage? What a dreary chronicle it contains of unremarkable people! But suddenly, while plodding through that long list, one is arrested by the vivid account of this one man, Jabez, who was "more honorable than his brothers".

What made him so honorable? We are told simply: he was a man of prayer; he "called upon the God of Israel". But surely among so many generations Jabez was not alone in prayer? Yes, there were many others who prayed; but not like Jabez. For scripture says of him, "God gave him what he asked!" Nor just a part, but all that he asked!

In any generation, a person who knows how to pray and get exactly what he or she requests from God will be honored indeed. Such people are not often found! Yet it need not be so. Jabez was not unusual in himself. He was an ordinary man who gained extraordinary favor with heaven simply because he learned the secret of powerful prayer. There is no good reason why you and I should not learn the same secret, and gain the same honor from God.

Our text shows us four things that made Jabez' prayers so effective -

HE PRAYED BOLDLY

> "He called upon the God of Israel, saying, 'Oh that you would keep me from harm, so that it might not hurt me!"

That seems to be a very selfish prayer, the kind one might expect from a spoilt child, but not from a mature adult. Its apparently whining plea for a pain-free life of comfort is offensive. But then one is even more offended to find that God granted his request! How could the Lord possibly do it? Surely he demands more toughness of spirit from us than Jabez seems to display?

But a further look at the prayer denies that first judgment. Far from being a self-indulgent cry for a pleasant, untroubled life, Jabez' prayer is a bold, breathtaking venture into faith.

The meaning of his name provides the key: "Jabez" means "pain", or "grief". We are told that "his mother named him 'Jabez', saying, 'Because I bore him in pain'." *What was that pain? We don't know. Perhaps a clue is found in the lack of mention of his father (in contrast with the many generations listed before Jabez). Perhaps he was a child of incest, or of adultery; perhaps the young woman's husband had died or deserted her about the time Jabez was born; or perhaps the birth was unusually difficult and caused her terrible suffering? Whatever the cause, from that time on all natural love departed from Jabez's mother. Every time she looked at her infant son she shrank from him with loathing. Seeing him, she could think only of pain, pain, pain - so she called him "Grief" or "Jabez".*

Now "Grief" was a peculiar and burdensome name to give to a boy. Even in our time it would be a cruel trick for a parent to play on a helpless child. In Bible days it was a thousand times worse. For in those days names were thought to have immense power over those who bore them. As the name was, so the person would be.

To us a name is little more than a social convenience or a legal necessity, a thing of cultural custom. We do not attribute any mystical power to a name, either to bless or to curse. Not so the ancients. To them a person and his name were one. There was a powerful bond between them. As his name, so the person would be, for good or ill. To give a baby a name redolent of prosperity, peace, wellbeing, was to ensure that child a happy future; but to give an evil-speaking name was to blight the child with misery. That is why Hebrew parents delighted to incorporate one or more of the names of God into the names of their children, or names that spoke of peace, righteousness, divine favor.

The principle of name and nature being indistinguishable is seen most strongly in God. All that God is, his Name is, where the Name is, there is God; all God's personality, power, glory, grace, riches, life, are embodied in his name. A glance through a concordance will show you many demonstrations of the indissoluble union between God and his Name.

For such reasons, then, it was unthinkable in ancient Israel to give an infant a name that would be a constant curse, dooming the child to misery and hurt. Note how swiftly Jacob changed the bitter name that Rachel in her sorrow had given to her new-born son. He changed her dying lament, "Son-of-my-anguish," to "Son-of-my-right-hand" (Genesis 35:16-18), replacing her curse with his blessing.

There was no one to change Jabez' name. His father was not there. So his mother took a fearful vengeance on him, and burdened him with "Grief" for the remainder of his life. From that day on, his life was shadowed by the bleakness of his mother's curse.

You might say, "That was only a foolish superstition." Perhaps it was, but in that time and place it had an irresistible power to be self-fulfilling. Those were primitive days, when no-one questioned the virulent strength of a curse. A mother's curse was viewed with special horror. In that environment, as in primitive societies today, curses had power to destroy a man's life. For example, if an Australian aborigine learns that a witchdoctor has "pointed the bone" at him, he will soon sicken and die, and rarely can anyone rescue him from the curse.

In a different way, yet not so different, people in modern society carry similar burdens. Perhaps they are born with some emotional, mental, or physical disability - congenitally cursed. Perhaps the way they were brought up has built many fears, traumas, weaknesses into them - cursed by their nurture. Perhaps certain social influences have shattered their confidence, eroded their strength, convinced them that life will always be fraught with misery and failure - cursed by their neighbors. And so on.

In any case, you can be sure that Jabez' name worked its hurt into him day after relentless day. There was no escape from his mother's baleful word. In that society, only his father, who either would not or could not, had power to change his name. So Jabez lived his days in misery.

Then somehow, on one of those sorrowful days, Jabez learned that while no man could help him, his God could. By heaven's grace the curse could be broken. He could become a new man, with a new destiny. He could seize a new prosperity. Under God, he could become master of his life and escape the prison of the past. He saw that God could do for him what no person could do: reach into his life and totally change it, inwardly and outwardly. He saw that nothing was too hard for God.

So he stormed heaven with a wonderful boldness of faith, "Oh that you would keep me from harm; protect me from my mother's curse. Don't let it harm me; break its power in my life!"

No longer does his prayer seem selfish. Suddenly we recognize it as a mighty affirmation of confidence in the creative, life-changing power of God. No wonder God gave him what he asked!

How about you? Do you have something in your life that hurts you day after day? Perhaps it is hereditary. Perhaps it was imposed upon you by your upbringing. Perhaps it is something society has built into you. Whatever, it is some weakness, or sin, or bondage, or curse, that haunts you and wounds you again and again. You may have despaired of ever being free. But Jabez shows that bold prayer can move God to break any chain and to make you into a new person!

HE PRAYED PERSISTENTLY

> *"He called upon the God of Israel, saying, `Oh that you would bless me indeed!"*

Almost every word of that sentence is significant. He called, not just on God, but on "the God of Israel"; *he prayed, not just for blessing, but* "for blessing indeed".

Do you see the link between this prayer and the familiar story of Jacob at the brook Jabbok (Genesis 32:22-30). There "Jacob", the cheat, the conniver, the cunning, became "Israel" - a prince with God, the man of prevailing faith. His name and destiny were changed. Notice how he gained this divine favor: he would not let go of God. Even when the Lord dislocated his hip, still he wrestled, despite the wrenching agony, crying through the pain and tears, "I will not let you go unless you bless me!" *What persistence! What courage! What tenacity! What passion! What determination! Then comes the truly amazing statement, made by God himself to Jacob,* "You have struggled with God and have overcome me!" *(verse 28). A man prevailed over the Almighty! God could not overpower the man! (verse 25). Not even the pummeling fist of God, disjointing his bones, could force Jacob to let go. He hung on until the blessing, the full blessing was his.*

Note again the parallel with Jabez. Surely his prayer was inspired by the memory of Jacob's experience. If Jacob the cheat could become Israel the prince by such persistent prayer, then he (Jabez), the man cursed by grief, could become instead highly favored. So he called on Jacob's God. He took up Jacob's prayer. He cried, as Jacob had done, "Bless me indeed!" *He would not let go until he knew that God had given him his heart's desire. And God gave him what he asked.*

There is power in persistent prayer. The kind of prayer that refuses to give up until it obtains the prize. The kind of prayer that casts off discouragement even when it seems that God himself is the enemy. Most people have forgotten how to pray like that. We get so many things so easily that we have lost the heart for lonely dauntless heroism in prayer.

That kind of praying, of course, is not always necessary. Sometimes, before you even ask, God hears (Isaiah 65:24). Prayer may be answered quickly, easily, joyfully, with neither struggle, pain, nor tears. But not always. If you are serious about becoming mighty in prayer, then you will probably find the Holy Spirit bringing you to your own Jabbok, where only dauntless persistence will prevail. Sometimes just a murmur of desire is enough to bring cascades of blessing. But just as surely there are other times when God seems to be our most implacable opponent, when faith is tried to the limit, when the steel has to enter our soul, when we are stretched to the limit of endurance. But if you have the heart of a Jacob or a Jabez, you will prevail! You will see greater things done through your prayers than you ever thought possible. You will join the company of those who are "more honorable" than their brothers!

Search the Psalms and you will soon find many examples of bewildered prayer, complaining that God is heedless of the cry of his people, or seems to have made himself their worst enemy. Scripture and life, both show that God does appear sometimes to be acting against us, or at least to be indifferent to our need. Consider Job. Note the reaction of his wife (2:9) - similar to the shaking fist you have possibly been tempted on occasions to raise against God! But then see Job's response (verse 10).

If you know that what you are asking lies within the promise of God to you, then you should refuse to be deterred by opposition, or by heaven's apparent deafness, or by seeming divine rejection, or by any other opponent, whether human, demonic, or angelic. Possess your possessions! Allow nothing to cheat you of the blessing you know is rightfully yours!

HE PRAYED EXPANSIVELY

> *"He called upon the God of Israel, saying, 'Oh that you would enlarge my borders!'"*

Here is a man asking for more! He had much, and he was thankful for what he had, but he wanted more! What happens to those who want more? Is God offended? Does such discontent irritate the Almighty? Will he get angry if you tell him you don't have enough? On the contrary, such extravagance of expectation is delightful to the Father. Did the Lord reject Jabez' prayer? No! He gave him what he asked: more*!*

Somehow a kind of self-abnegating piety has developed in the church, abject in its humiliation and self-deprecation, convinced that it deserves nothing from God and should expect nothing. Much modern devotion is characterized by this fatalistic passivism - the idea that we have no right to insist upon God doing anything for us; that we must humbly accept whatever portion the Lord pleases to give us. Let him give what he will (they say); let him take what he will; we make no demands upon his generosity or grace.

Those downcast eyes do have an appearance of godliness; but in reality such abjectness is far distant from the aggressive, confident, vigorous faith that scripture everywhere commends. Note, however, that, "aggressive" is not the same as "arrogant". We are surely required to walk humbly before the Lord, recognizing our utter dependence upon his mercy and grace. But neither is humility the same as inactivity. Humble we must be; but inactive, helpless, passive, fatalistic, we must not be. We are called to arise, to go, to believe, to do! (See Mark 16:14-18; and many other arousing references.)

How can anyone hold a Bible in their hand, and then wonder whether God wants to do great things for those who believe? You will search in vain in scripture for the prostrated helplessness that some churches encourage. Everywhere you turn you will find instead exhortations to stand up, to be bold, to call upon the Lord with vigorous faith, confident that he will do wondrous things.

Meditate on the following promises of answered prayer: Matthew 6:6; 7:7-11; 18:19-20; 21:21-22; Mark 11:24-25; John 14:13-14; 15:7, 16; 16:23-24; Romans 10:12-13; Ephesians 3:20; Hebrews 4:16; 1 John 3:22; 5:14. Those are but a few of the promises. You could without difficulty find as many more, especially in the Old Testament.

So you have not yet received from God more than a small part of what he wants to give you. Expand your faith! Ask God to "enlarge your borders." *You may be surprised at how much he will give you!*

HE PRAYED SUBMISSIVELY

> *"He called upon God of Israel, saying, 'Oh that your hand would be with me!'"*

There is a controversy in the Church today between those who belong to what is called the "faith movement" and those who denounce them. On the one side are those who teach the principles of "name it and claim it ... confess it and possess it"; on the other side are those who reckon that such ideas are heresy.

It seems to me that both groups are in error: the one, because they expect too much; the other, because they expect too little. Jabez had a better balance, expressed in his two phrases: enlarge my borders *and* keep your hand upon me. *Some people, however, are only on the side of those who boldly pray, "enlarge my borders"; while others are only on the side of those who humbly plead, "keep your hand upon me."* Yet those sayings are not "contradictory" ideas, but "complementary". How can there be an argument between mighty faith and humble submission? There should be no such quarrel. Indeed, only those who are deeply submitted to the Father's will (as say, Jesus was), can truly have mountain-moving faith (as Jesus did).

Think also about this: you can only pray "according to God's will" when you are "claiming his promise". There is no such thing as a prayer of faith without trust in the promise of God; and no prayer can please God without faith! (Hebrews 11:6)

To place no limit at all on prayer is just as wrong as to abandon believing prayer altogether. To adopt an attitude of supine fatalism is surely as foolish as behaving with greedy presumption. If some in the "faith" camp are too materialistic, some in the other camp are too "spiritual". If some are too bold, others are too submissive. More balance is needed - the kind shown by Jabez. He refused to place himself in a camp that had only one prayer, whether that was "enlarge my border", or "keep your hand on me". He held both petitions in tension together.

Likewise, we need to understand how to pray "expansively" - expecting great things from God; but also how to pray "submissively" - content to stay within the boundaries of God's will. Once again mark it: faith, real faith, cannot function outside the parameters of the divine purpose. So we need to echo Jabez' prayer that God will keep us in the centre of his will; yet also recognize that within those lines there is abundant scope to expect mighty miracles from God.

Consider Paul, and other key people in scripture. What great things God did for them! But it is equally true that there were many things God would not do for them - things that would have harmed his purpose. So the Lord, for example, refused (at least for a time) to take away Paul's "thorn in the flesh"; *neither would the Lord have allowed Paul to develop his tent-making skills into a great commercial enterprise. All the "faith-confession" in the world could not have persuaded God to allow that business to prosper. He had other plans for Paul! Similarly, Paul was not free to "claim by faith" great personal wealth, or a magnificent retirement villa in the country, or any one of a hundred other things that are innocent in themselves but would have been a hindrance to his apostolic ministry. In brief, nothing was available to Paul as an answer to prayer that was not fully consistent with the task God had given him to do. Yet Paul did not lack opportunity to pray, to believe, and to see many astonishing miracles.*

Again, consider the greatest "faith-man" of them all, Jesus himself. Who ever had faith in God remotely comparable to his? Yet the same rule holds. There were many mighty things the Father was willing to do for Jesus. There were many more things the Father could not do for him. Was there ever any conflict between those two parts of his walk with God? Of course not! Great as his faith was, still greater was Christ's submission to the Father's will (Hebrews 10:7).

You should do the same. As nearly as you can, discover first your place in the will of God. What is his purpose for you? What boundaries has he built around you? Are there parameters that determine if it is appropriate for God to do some things for you, but not others? Once you have a sense of what God wants you to do or be, then you will know what the focus of your prayer should be.

This does not limit prayer so much as define it. You cannot pray in faith until you know what God's promise is; but his promise is variable, different for each one of us, dependent upon each person's life perimeter. God will give me things that he will not give you; and vice versa. There are, of course, many promises that belong equally to every child of God. But there are many others uniquely shaped to each person's part in God's plan.

Thus defined, the balance we are seeking is to ask only for those things that are consonant with the Father's particular will for each one of us. Nonetheless, there will still be such scope for faith, such abundance of opportunity, such promised blessing, within the boundaries of God's plan for you and me that none of us will even begin to exhaust what the Father is willing to give in response to our eager expectation!

CONCLUSION

The goal is set before us of not being outdone by Jabez. Think how great are our advantages in relation to his! How much Bible did Jabez have? Only a small part of what you and I call scripture. We have the gospel, plus personal union with Christ, the fullness of the Holy Spirit, the fellowship of the saints, a thousand more promises, and on, and on. It would be our shame if we could not touch the throne of God more nearly, more forcefully, more effectively than that honorable man of old! So let us reach for the highest! (Philippians 3:12-16) Surely, if Jabez could achieve such renown in the annals of heaven, so can you and I. Indeed, if Jabez, gained this encomium, that he was "the more-honorable Jabez", *we should receive the fame of being* "much-more-honorable"*!*

The secret lies in building the same four qualities into your praying that Jabez built into his.

Those who thus pray will have the same testimony as Jabez, "God gave them what they asked!" *Truly, such people know how to* "possess their possessions"!

POINTS TO PONDER

(1) What harm did Jabez suffer all his life until the moment of his great prayer? Think about ways in which people today are similarly afflicted.

(2) Jabez gained a revelation of God that changed his concept of prayer. What was that revelation, and how did he gain it?

(3) What special significance did names have in Bible days, and how did their concept of a name differ from ours?

(4) What did God do to discourage Jacob's insistent prayer? Does God often act so discouragingly? Can you cite any other biblical or modern examples?

(5) Which man in the Bible fought with and overcame God? Is there an example there for us?

(6) Does answered prayer always require a prolonged and bitter struggle?

(7) What is the fault of much modern piety?

(8) Meditate in the promises of answered prayer given above. Find other such promises in your Bible.

(9) Is there a contradiction between "claiming the promise" of God and praying "according to his will"?

(10) What is the proper balance in prayer that we should try to maintain?

(11) Think about some of the things that God could not have given to, say, Paul, no matter how hard the apostle had "believed" for them. How does that principle apply to yourself?

(12) If Jabez was more honourable than his brothers, should we strive to be more honourable than Jabez?

WHY PEOPLE DON'T PRAY

In the Forest Lawn gardens in Los Angeles there is a statue of General George Washington. On the statue is an inscription, describing Washington at Valley Forge -

> "With his lean, ragged levies, undismayed he crouched among the vigilant hills; a show to the disdainful, heaven-blinded foe. Undaunted, unsupported, disobeyed, thwarted, maligned, conspired against, betrayed - yet nothing could unheart him. Wouldst thou know his secret? There, in that thicket, on the snow, Washington knelt before his God, and prayed."[4]

Thus have great men and women often proven in the heat of conflict the immense value of prayer. But if that is so, then why don't more people pray? The Father's lament must still be the same as it was long ago -

> *"Why have you stopped calling upon me, O Jacob? Why have you grown weary of me, O Israel?"*[5]

Plainly, when you examine prayer, nothing much has changed across the centuries! Yet in answer to the Lord's query, we can suggest some reasons for the prayerlessness of his people -

---

[4] Canon R. G. Sutherland.
[5] Is 43:22.

Part One -
THINGS THAT HINDER PRAYER

DISOBEDIENCE TO GOD

Some Christians simply have a disobedient spirit. They refuse to do what God has commanded them to do. To that there is but one antidote: *repentance*!

Others perhaps, are not aware that the command to pray is imperative. They should open their eyes and see, and unstop their ears and hear. Prayer is not an optional extra; rather, it is a mandatory part of a godly life.

> "You are to look closely at this command and stress it that you do not consider prayer an optional work and act, as if it were enough that others pray. You should know that prayer is earnestly enjoined, with the threat of God's supreme displeasure and punishment if it is neglected ... He who does not do this should know that he is no Christian and does not belong to the kingdom of God."[6]

Therefore, we are commanded to pray:

- <u>*at all times*</u> (Luke 18:1; 1 Thessalonians 5:17-18)

- <u>*in all places*</u> (see Psalm 61:1-2)

- <u>*in all circumstances*</u> (see Psalm 55:16-17)

- <u>*for all needs*</u> (see Philippians 4:6)

Secondly, people hold back from prayer because of a

LACK OF CONFIDENCE

At heart, many Christians doubt that prayer is truly effective. They think of it as a kind of pious exercise, but they have little or no assurance that prayer is a

---

[6] Martin Luther; from What Luther Says, compiled by E. M. Plass; Concordia Pub. House, St Louis, MO, 1959; vol 2, selection # 1075

mighty force that can move mountains. Yet there are scores of promises of answered prayer in scripture. Let them all be summed up in this one, which is probably the single most extraordinary statement on the power of prayer in the Bible -

> *"This is my first instruction: let petitions, requests, intercessions, and thanksgiving be made for everyone; especially for the emperor and all other rulers, so that we may live peacefully and quietly, full of godliness and integrity" (1 Timothy 2:1-3).*

The "emperor" mentioned by Paul was Nero, who was a "monster of cruelty"; yet the apostle wished him to be prayed for, believing that prayer could change even the worst of men. Likewise, the church Fathers universally encouraged such prayers; not even the fiercest persecution could deter them. Thus Origen wrote:

> "We do, when occasion requires, give help to kings, and that, so to say, a divine help, 'putting on the whole armor of God.' And this we do in obedience to the injunction of the apostle, 'I exhort, therefore, that first of all, supplications, prayers, intercessions, and giving of thanks, be made for all men; for kings, and for all that are in authority;' *and the more anyone excels in piety, the more effective help does he render to kings, even more than is given by soldiers, who go forth and slay as many of the enemy as they can ... And as we by our prayers vanquish all demons who stir up war, and lead to the violation of oaths, and disturb the peace, we in this way are much more helpful to the king than those who go into the field and fight for them ... And none fight better for the king than we do ... (for) we fight on his behalf, forming a special army - an army of piety - by offering our prayers to God."*[7]

Did you notice the implied threat in Origen's words: that the prayers of the church could destroy kings as well as save them? Indeed, the early Christians believed that this happened often:

- ♦ <u>Nero</u> began to persecute the church in A.D. 64, and used Christians as living torches to illuminate his palace garden parties. Within 3½ years he was dead by his own hand, loathed by all.[8]

---

[7] Uagainst Celsus Bk 8, ch 73. Written c. 245.

[8] Except the Greeks, to whom he had shown remarkable favor, hence the Nero Redivivus legend

- <u>Septimius Severus</u> began to harm the church during the first decade of the third century; he died in 211, worn out by sickness, and broken in spirit.

- <u>Decius</u> (under whose persecution Origen himself was tortured several times) instituted the first empire-wide and fully sanctioned persecution, but was then dead within two years, killed in battle by the Goths.

- <u>Valerian</u> in 258 began a particularly fierce persecution, but within two years he was captured by the Parthians and held prisoner until his death, around 269.

The procession of disasters that befell the persecuting emperors was so extraordinary, that in 311, Galerius, the last of the pagan emperors, who had begun by inflicting many miseries upon the church, but who was now terminally ill, from his sick-bed issued a plea for all Christians to pray for him![9]

Thus the early Christians demonstrated the power of prayer to change the face of nations, to subdue unrighteousness, to strengthen the church to confront and to overcome all her enemies. It would be difficult to find a more extraordinary witness.

Here then is a good reason to pray, pray often, and pray persistently: nothing is impossible for the man or woman of prayer!

A third reason for carelessness in prayer arises from

WRONG PRIORITIES

No time for prayer? Too busy? Waiting for a more convenient opportunity? You will always be "too busy"! There will always be many distractions! John Donne had a comment on this problem -

> "I throw myself down in my Chamber, and I call in, and invite God, and his Angels thither, and when they are there, I neglect God and his Angels for the noise of a fly, for the rattling of a coach, for the whining of a door!"[10]

> "A memory of yesterday's pleasures, a fear of tomorrow's dangers, a straw under my knee, a noise in mine ear, a light in mine eye, an anything, a nothing, a fancy, a Chimera in my

---

[9] See Eusenius 8:17; also Lactantius, anti-Nicene Fathers 7/13 ch 33,34.
[10] From a sermon preached 12/12/1626.

brain, troubles me in my prayer. So certainly is there nothing, nothing in spiritual things, perfect in this world."[11]

You must have encountered the same problem. No sooner do you resolve to pray than a thousand hindrances intervene to prevent you from getting started. The devil raises countless interruptions; your own thoughts rush in upon you tumultuously; other "more urgent" tasks demand your time and attention; everything seems easier, or more necessary than prayer!

Such disturbances must be resisted and overcome; fix the time when you intend to pray, and then stick to it, not allowing yourself to be enticed away except for the most truly compelling reasons.

Yet there is a counterbalance: sometimes our best prayer is done by being diligent in labor rather than on our knees; a fact that Luther himself admits -

> "But there can be works that are as good or better than a prayer, particularly when need requires them. Thus a statement attributed to St Jerome says: 'All the works of believers are prayer.' And there is a proverb: 'The faithful worker offers a double prayer' ... "[12]

No one has better exemplified this principle than Brother Lawrence, a 17th century saint, renowned as the man who more than any other lived constantly in the presence of God. He was first a soldier, then, after he was wounded, a footman, but was dismissed from service as "a great awkward fellow who broke everything." Later, when he was past fifty years of age, he entered the Carmelite Order in Paris, and was employed as a kitchen worker. He disliked the work, but persevered in it for thirty years, until his death (in 1691), and made it a vehicle of devotion to God. His aim, which those who knew him best reckoned he had accomplished, was to be as much in the presence of God at the kitchen sink as in the chapel, and to be motivated in all things by love for God.

One of Brother Lawrence's great precepts was that every act done in the name of the Lord was a prayer. Thus it was said of him -

> "With him, the time of prayer was not different from any other; he had set times for it, which the Father Prior had appointed, but he neither wanted nor asked for them, for the

---

[11] From a sermon preached 2/29/1627. <u>Chimera</u> comes from a Greek myth about a fire-breathing she-monster with a lion's head, a goat's body, and a serpent's tail; it now means a wild illusion in the mind, or perhaps an unreasonable dream or fancy.

[12] Ibid. compare also the testimony of Brother Lawrence, also given above - see the footnote immediately following this one

most absorbing work did not divert him from God ... He had never been able to pray according to a pattern as some do ... He was more united with God during his ordinary activities than in religious exercises, in which he was generally afflicted with spiritual dryness ... He found that the best way of reaching God was through (his) ordinary occupations ... (He thought) it a great delusion to imagine that prayer-time should be different from any other, for we are equally bound to be united to God by work at work-time as by prayer at prayer-time."[13]

Let nothing then supplant prayer as the first priority of your life - yet withal recognize that there are many ways to pray.

A more serious reason for failure to pray lies in the sad fact that many Christians have

NO SENSE OF DESTINY

"Stay alert at all times, and pray that God will help you to escape all those things that are going to happen, and that you will be worthy to stand in the presence of the Son of Man" (Luke 21:36).

Everywhere in the church you can find people who live only for today. They have no vision of the great hour that lies ahead of us, when Christ will return in his glory, and all the holy angels with him, and we will be caught up to meet him in the air. They do not tremble at the thought of the judgments that must one day fall upon the earth. They never ask: "What will happen to me if Christ were to return today?"

Jesus said that people with a sense of the destiny for which God has appointed them will be people of prayer. They know that prayer is the one sure barricade against being trapped in the ruin that will overwhelm the nations. They know that prayer alone will so unite them with Christ that his appearance will hold for them no terror, but only measureless joy!

---

[13] The Practice of the Presence of God; Brother Lawrence of the Resurrection; tr. By Donald Attwater; Burns & Oats, London; 1977; pg. 37,39,45, 48-49. Other similar sayings are scattered through the book.

Then there are those who do not pray because of

LACK OF LOVE

Prayer is an effective thermometer of the level of warmth of our love for God and for our neighbor - see 1 Samuel 12:23; and compare also Ephesians 6:18-19. How could those who love God not find delight in conversing with him? How could those who love the people around them not pray for the Lord to shower his grace upon them?

But perhaps the most common reason why people do not pray, is because they think

PRAYER IS TOO HARD

People have an impression that successful prayer requires tedious, arduous, and passionate hours. No doubt there is some truth in that perception -

> "At times I, who teach this and prescribe it to others, have learned from my own example that praying comes close to being the most difficult of all our works ... What the holy Fathers have said is true: there is no greater work than praying. Mumbling with the mouth is easy. But to follow the words with earnestness of heart in deep devotion ... is a great deed in the eyes of God ... To pray aright is a difficult task, and the art supreme ... People who are experienced in spiritual matters have said that no labor is comparable to the labor of praying."[14]

Scripture itself shows that there are times when prayer does demand the utmost we can give:

- *Moses*, moved by Israel's sin, lay prostrate before the Lord, fasting, 40 days and 40 nights (Deuteronomy 9:18,25).

- *Samuel* cried to the Lord all night, angry, when he learned that Saul had been rejected by God (1 Samuel 15:11)

- *Ezra* was appalled at the mixed marriages the people had embraced, and he sat in sackcloth, ashes, and tears, plucking out his hair, all day (9:3-5); then, at the time of the evening sacrifice, he cast himself on his face before the house of God, weeping, confessing, praying (10:1)

---

[14] Ibid., # 1081, 1088.

- Nehemiah "sat down and wept, and mourned for days, and ... continued fasting and praying" when he heard that the walls of Jerusalem were still in ruins (1:4-6)

- Daniel "turned his face to the Lord, seeking him by prayer and supplications, with fasting and sackcloth, and ashes," for the captivity of Judah to end (9:3).

Hence we are taught to persist in prayer: Isaiah 62:1,6-7; Luke 18:1-7; 11:5-10

Nonetheless, in all those examples the actual *prayers* seem to have been brief; in fact, the scriptures do encourage brevity in prayer. For example, note that the Lord's Prayer in the original Greek text is just 73 words (Matthew 6:9-13). The same can be said of Elijah's powerful prayer on Mt Carmel (1 Kings 18:36,37); plus Ecclesiastes 5:2; Matthew 6:7-8).[15] Even the most passionate of the Psalms are comparatively brief, encompassing even life-and-death prayers within only a few verses.

Why should it be otherwise? Do we not have copious promises of answered prayer given to us in scripture? Has not the Lord promised a willing ear to our requests? Therefore long, tedious, repetitious prayers may be a sign of unbelief rather than of faith. They often stem from a hidden opinion that God is a tight-fisted miser, parsimonious, reluctant to grant even a mild petition, begrudging every morsel of blessing we pry out of his firmly closed hand. That is hardly the Bible picture of the Lord of all Generosity!

Those who understand the swiftness of the Father to catch every prayer breathed by his children know that our best praying is probably done when we learn how to *"pray without ceasing"*,[16] that is, when we maintain a constant dialogue with God in the midst of every activity.

Jesus himself castigated *"vain repetition"* in prayer,[17] as though God will be more likely to answer multiplied pleas than to grant just one. What nonsense! In general, the fewer the words, the better the prayer. It is more heathen than Christian to go on and on, as if God were asleep, or absent, or uncaring, like some pagan idol. Leave that godless babble to the priests of Baal; we should rather follow the example of Elijah, who called down fire from heaven with less than forty words!

---

[15] Note that in Gethsemane, Jesus was struggling, not to change the Father's mind, but to bring himself to submission to the Father's will

[16] 1 Th 5:17

[17] Mt 6:7-13

The lesson is: change your expectations, and you will probably get great answers to brief prayers just as well as to long ones! However, there is of course no limit on *praise* nor on *communion* with the Father. It should be no hardship to linger in the presence of God, rejoicing in his love, reveling in his fellowship, revering his glorious majesty. But when you have something to ask from the Lord, then speak up firmly and concisely; present your request, and then be content to leave the matter in his hands. Countless empty phrases can hardly add any strength to your petition - especially when you heap them all together at the one time. We are encouraged each day to come back to the Father and to ask for the "bread" we need for that day - but you need only ask once!

CONCLUSION

Talk to anyone who has rich experience in prayer, and you will find them echoing the words of the psalmist -

> *"The Lord stays close beside everyone who calls upon him, especially those who pray with sincerity and integrity. Those who reverence the Lord will be given their deepest desires, for he will hear their cry and hasten to deliver them. The Lord never turns away his eye, nor takes his hand away from those who love him" (Psalm 145:18-19).*

Ivan Turgenev (1818-1883) once gave a pungent definition of prayer: "Whatever a man prays for, he prays for a miracle. Every prayer reduces itself to this: `Great God, grant that twice two be not four!'"

May the Lord give us such boldness in prayer that we too disturb the mathematics of the universe, as we enforce his will upon the kingdom of darkness and among the nations!

Part Two - BEYOND PAGAN PRAYER

> *"We are not seeking to commend ourselves, O Lord, nor are we looking for others to praise us; rather, we yearn only to see your name made glorious through a demonstration of your love and faithfulness. But our hearts are broken, because the heathen stand there mocking us: `Where is your God?'"*[18]

The psalmist declares the vanity of pagan gods (vs 4-7), and he insists that those who worship such idols will themselves be made helpless (vs 8). But how can that be proved? There is only one way: show that the true God, unlike the gods of the heathen, is alive in the heavens, and able to do on earth anything he pleases (vs. 3). Yet the psalmist has a problem. It was this: the heathen could see little difference between Israel and her neighbors in this matter of getting answers to prayer. The psalmist bravely declared that his God works miracles, while the gods of the heathen are deaf, dumb, and lifeless; but the ungodly did not agree.

"Where then *is* your God?" they jeered. "You say that your God answers prayer; but so do the gods we worship! In fact we think our gods do a better job of it than yours does!"

The people of Israel also, often subjugated under a foreign tyrant, made the pawn of a succession of great empires, must have felt that Yahweh was a feeble deity, with little strength against the mighty gods who gave the heathen so many riches and such great strength.

The psalmist knew that was false. He knew the pagan idols were only wood and stone, utterly helpless to answer prayer, or to do anything; but he longed for the Lord God to prove it by a display of his limitless power. *"Not for our sake,"* he cried, *"nor for our glory, but to glorify your own great name among the nations, please, O Lord, show your loving faithfulness and do marvelous things for us! Then the heathen will have to admit that you alone are God!"*

The heathen, however, were ready to admit nothing of the sort. As far as they could see, their gods were as good as, if not better than, the God of Israel. Their idols seemed to answer prayer just as often and just as effectively as Yahweh did.

---

[18] Ps 115:1-2

Does that surprise you? Look at these examples from the past. They are testimonies of answered prayer culled from various pagan sources-

Babylon (600 BC)

"O heroic one, Ishtar, immaculate one of the goddesses ... The goddess *Lady of Heaven* ... O Ishtar ... you rule the heavens ... You alter the Fates, and an ill event becomes good ... At your right (hand) is Justice; at your left (hand) is Goodness ... How good it is to pray to you, how blessed to be heard by you! ... Have pity on me, O Ishtar! Order my prospering! Glance on me in affirmation! Accept my litany!"[19]

Greece (400 BC)

"The acquisition of wealth in the form of money and property, much like success in agriculture, was under the influence of the gods. One could pray for it for the members of one's family (Isaeus 8:15-16), and one could include it in a curse ... (Indeed) the acquisition and preservation of wealth seem generally to fall into the category of good fortune resulting from the goodwill of the gods (Dem 1:10-11). But lest we think divine influence in this area was too vague to be meaningful, Xenophon, who in 399 had become so impoverished that he had to sell his horse for money for the trip home, heeded a soothsayer's warning that his poverty resulted from neglect of Zeus Meilichios. He quickly sacrificed to Zeus Meilichios, and his financial fortunes took a dramatic and lasting turn for the better (Ada 7:8:1-6) ...

"The most immediate examples of divine intervention are those found in the cult of the healing god Asclepius. This immediacy is suggested by the experience which Ambrosia, an Athenian woman, had at his sanctuary in Epidaurus (*IG* IV² 121, lines 33-41):

'Ambrosia from Athens, blind in one eye. She came as a supplicant to Asclepius. As she walked about in the sanctuary she laughed at some of the cures, thinking it unbelievable and impossible, that, for example, the lame and blind became well

---

[19] The Greatness That Was Babylon, pg 327

merely by having a dream. But when she went to sleep she had a dream. The god seemed to stand over her and say that he would make her healthy, but in repayment she must erect in the sanctuary a silver pig as a memorial of her folly. And after the god had said this he seemed to tear open her diseased eye and to pour in some drug. And when day came Ambrosia went out healthy' ...

"There were times in their lives when all individuals, and not just the superstitious, privately performed sacrifices and directed prayers to the gods. In times of personal need for health, safety, money, and such things, individuals personally made sacrifices, uttered prayers, and erected dedications.

"In general terms the Athenians believed that piety was a necessary, though not sufficient, cause of national and personal prosperity. The vast majority of Athenians would have agreed, I think, both with Antiphon (6:5) when he claimed that 'a man who acts impiously and transgresses against the gods would deprive himself of the very hopes which are the greatest good men have,' and with Isocrates (15:281-282) when he exhorted the Greeks 'to think that those who get more from the gods both now and in the future are those who are most pious and most diligent in their tendance of the gods.'"[20]

Rome

Valerius, a Roman hero of the 4th century BC, when he was military tribune, was obliged to engage with a giant Gaul in single combat. The tribune was being worsted until a raven settled on the Gaul's helmet, distracting his attention, which allowed Valerius to deliver the death blow. The tribune was certain it was an answer to prayer, and he at once gave thanks to the gods. As an act of grateful memoriam he adopted the cognomen *"Corvus"* (Raven).[21]

Cato, a wealthy landowner and political leader of the 3rd century BC instructed his son to offer the following prayer for his farm -

"Father Mars, I pray and beseech thee that thou mayest be

---

[20] Athenian Popular Religion, by Jon D. Mikalsom; Univ of N. Carolina press; 1983; pg 24, 55-56, 89, 104. Many inscriptions and dedicatory prayers have been preserved, giving thanks to various gods for what the petitioners took to be divine answers to prayer.

[21] Livey, Bk 7.26.4

propitious and well-disposed to me, to our home and household, for which cause I have ordered the offering of pig, sheep, and ox to be led around my field, my land, and my farm, that thou might prevent, ward off, and avert diseases, visible and invisible, barrenness and waste, accident and bad water, that thou wouldest permit the crop and fruit of the earth, the vines and shrubs to wax great and prosper, that thou wouldest preserve the shepherds and their flocks in safety and give prosperity and health to me and our house and household ... for all these causes ... be increased by the sacrifice of this offering of sucking pig, lamb, and calf."[22]

Caesar Augustus, after a glorious military victory declared -

"I have achieved all my hopes; what else am I to pray the immortal gods to give me except that I should be permitted to enjoy their unanimous support until the very end of my life?"[23]

The Romans carefully structured their prayers, both public and private. They developed complex forms and liturgies, and were so meticulous in their performance that if a mistake were made, even of only one word in the liturgy, they did not hesitate to begin the entire performance again, even though enormous expense might be involved. They would hardly have been so painstaking if they had not believed in the efficacy of properly offered prayers.

A special part of the Roman practice of prayer was the offering of a sacrifice. There were two kinds:

- ♦ those offered in conjunction with a prayer to gain the god's favour; and

- ♦ those offered in gratitude after a prayer was answered.

Literally thousands of inscriptions are still extant, recording both kinds of oblation.[24]

Added to the above, many other examples could be given from many people who believe in and practice prayer. Thus we could refer again to the Greeks:

" ... the individual shares in the benefits and the losses which

---

[22] The Romans & Their Gods, pg 30.

[23] Ibid, pg 33.

[24] Ibid, pg 37.

result from divine intervention in matters of the state. But the individual also has concerns quite apart from those of the state as a whole, and he may well have felt the intervention of the gods in these areas more acutely. Xenophon puts into the mouth of Ischomachus a fairly comprehensive list of those matters in which one felt the need of divine assistance in his personal life:

'I begin by giving service to the gods and I attempt to act in such a way that it may be right for me, as I pray, to find health, strength of body, honor in the city, goodwill among friends, honorable safety in war, and wealth which is increased honorably.'

"The belief that divine assistance availed the individual in these aspects of his life is not unique to Ischomachus or Xenophon, and reference to most elements of the list can be found elsewhere in our sources."[25]

The same kind of testimony can be found in writings from the Orient -

"The deity of Koto no Mama deserves the trust that people put in him. I enjoy knowing that this is the shrine 'where every prayer's been glibly answered' by the god."[26]

"The deity of Aridoshi. It was past his shrine that Tsurayuki was riding when his horse was taken ill, and he was told that this was due to the anger of the god. He then dedicated a poem to the god, whereupon his horse was cured - a delightful incident."[27]

---

[25] Athenian Popular Religion, pg 22; see also 23,24.

[26] The pillow Book of Sei Shonagon; tr. By Ivan Morris; penguin Classics 1967; pg 207. Footnote #456 (pg 345) state; "This can mean literally 'prayers that are fully answered'. The basis is a punning poem that starts; 'This is indeed a shrine/Where every prayers been glibly answered (by the god)."

[27] Ibid. Footnote #457 (page 355) says: "In the collected works of KI no Tsurayuki we read that one day, when he was riding back to the capital, his horse suddenly became ill. The local inhabitants informed him, 'This is the doing of the god who dwells in these parts. For all these many years he always lets people know of his existence.' Since Tsurayuki had no suitable offering to present to the irate deity, he simply washed his hands (to acquire ritual purity) 'and facing the hill, where no sign of the god existed,' dedicated the following poem to him: 'How could I have known/that in this cloudy, unfamiliar sky/ there dwelt the Passage of the Ants?' Thereupon the god, appeased by this belated recognition of his existence, promptly restored the poet's horse to health."

So now we too, like the psalmist, have a problem: *how can we explain those reports?* That the heathen think at least some of their prayers are answered cannot be doubted. But what is the source of those answers? Several solutions come quickly to mind:

- perhaps demonic power is involved in at least some cases, especially where the presumed "answer" has dark ramifications.

- the sovereignty of God no doubt played some part. For example, Cyrus presumably praised his own gods for his extraordinary triumphs, but the prophets saw it differently (Isaiah 45:1-3).

- the same might be said of Nebuchadnezzar's irresistible conquests; in several places the prophets say he was raised up by God to be a hammer of divine judgment against the nations, including Israel; yet Nebuchadnezzar himself undoubtedly thought his conquests were given to him by Bel, the great god of Babylon.

- the mercy of God was probably at work, causing him to overlook ignorance and to respond to sincere worship and devotion (cp. Acts 17:29-30; also 10:34-35). An example of such a devout man, but one who did know the true God, can be found in Quintus Symmachus, who was one of the last great pagan apologists (c. 340 - c. 402). An orator and a consul, he pleaded with the Romans not to forget their ancestral gods, and made this rather moving comment:

    "Everything is full of God. Whatever we worship, it can fairly be called one and the same. We all look up to the same stars; the same heaven is above us all; the s`me universe surrounds every one of us. What does it matter by what system of knowledge each one of us seeks the truth? It is not by a single path that we attain to so great a secret."[28]

God, of course, is not concerned about whether or not we know *about* him, but that we *know* him; he is moved by love for our fallen state and yearns for our salvation. But Symmachus did express a sincere recognition of the spiritual dimension and a genuine sense of worship, as many other pagans did, and which God may well have desired to honor.

But having said all that, the main source of "answered prayer" among the heathen must simply have been *coincidence*. That is, when very large numbers of people

---

[28] The Romans and Their Gods, pg 124, 125.

pray there are bound to be enough accidental "answers" to prayer to encourage them to believe that they were heard by the gods.

But that at once brings us to the real problem, the sad fact that the experience of many Christians is hardly better than that of the pagans. So many of God's people are content with a level of answered prayer that could as well be coincidence as divine intervention. I mean, if you take 1000 of those Christians and 1000 pagans, the incidence of good and bad things experienced by them would probably not be significantly different.

Yet how can we be satisfied with a level of answered prayer that is well below the promise of God, or with answers that are hardly better than coincidence, or that spring only from occasional acts of divine sovereignty and mercy? Even worse, many Christians justify the paucity of answered prayer theologically, arguing for a passive submission to the will of God. The value of answered prayer, they say, is internal and subjective, it does not produce any objective change in the outer world; the prayer becomes its own end; the mere act of praying cleanses the soul and brings submission to God. But when that stage is reached, Christians are closer, say, to the Koran than they are to the Bible. Islam adopts the safe idea of disclaiming prayer as a means of securing the active intervention of God in daily human affairs. The devout Muslim could not echo the words of the Lord's Prayer, "Give me ... this, or that." Prayer to a Muslim is nothing more than a fatalistic submission to the inscrutable will of Allah.

But we are not Muslims; we are Christians! Our Bible contains a breathtaking array of promises of God's bounty and blessing.[29]

How should we respond to those promises?

The psalmist mentioned at the beginning of this chapter sets a good example. Like him, let us be ashamed of enjoying no better success in prayer than the heathen do. He began by mocking the heathen and saying their gods were worthless; but the heathen spoke back to Israel and said the same thing, *"Where then is your God?"* They reckoned that Yahweh was no more powerful to answer prayer than were their own gods. Their mockery was unendurable to the psalmist. He resolved to silence their jeers. He knew that resolute faith, persistent prayer, would arouse the Lord. He boldly affirmed: "The Lord *will* remember us, and he *will* bless us!" He waxed eloquent, and extravagant; he was expecting great things-

> *"The Lord will bless the House of Israel, and the House of Aaron; he will bless everyone who fears the Lord, whether they are small or great!" (vs. 12).*

---

[29] Mt 6:6; 7:7-11; 18:19-20; 21:21-22; Mk 11:24,25; Jn 14:13,14; 15:7,16; 16:23-24; Ro 10:12,13; Ep 3:20; He 4:16; 1 Jn 3:22; 5:14; plus many others.

How this world would change, how our churches would change, if all Christians were to become truly powerful in prayer! The challenge is before us to rise up in faith and meet the promise of God with a mighty expectation of divine action! We should achieve a level of answered prayer that cannot be mistaken for mere coincidence; a level of answered prayer that would be impossible without the input of irresistible faith!

POINTS TO PONDER

(1) Would you agree with Martin Luther that "he who neglects prayer is no Christian and does not belong to the kingdom of God"?

(2) How seriously did the early church take injunction to "pray for the emperor", *and what were the consequences?*

(3) Brother Lawrence "found that the best way of reaching God was through his ordinary occupations". Has that been your experience? Does effective prayer always require a formal time of petition, kneeling alone with God?

(4) Have you learned "to be as much in the presence of God at the kitchen sink as in the chapel"?

(5) What part does prayer play in relation to the last days and the return of Christ?

(6) What effect does Christian love, or the lack of it, have upon one's prayer life?

(7) Are long prayers ever commended in scripture? Which does scripture more encourage: long, or short prayers?

(8) How did Israel's experience of answered prayer compare with that of her pagan neighbours? Is there something you should learn from this comparison?

(9) How can we explain the apparent answers to prayer that the heathen declared their gods had given them?

(10) In what way does the Christian concept of prayer differ from that of Islam?

PRAISE YOUR WAY TO VICTORY!

One of the great ideas the Holy Spirit has restored to the church in our day is the power of praise. People are again hearing that the right kind of praise can liberate them from every bondage and bring them into an exciting new dimension of victorious, joyful, and fruitful living. This 20th-century rediscovery of an old biblical truth has produced two extreme reactions:

- the first denies that praise can do anything;

- the second insists that praise can do everything.

The former refuse to believe that such a simple act as praising God can have any real effect on a material problem; the latter are so sure of the miracle-working ability of praise they allow no limits to its accomplishments. Indeed, there are some who say the demand for praise is so absolute that no other response to life's crises is ever permitted by God. They claim that the secret of mountain-moving faith is to praise God for everything that happens to you, no matter what it might be. If your spouse is an alcoholic, if your daughter is raped, if your son turns to crime, if your house is burned down, if you are stricken with cancer - for all such things, for everything, for anything, you should (it is said) praise God!

What should we do with such claims?

THE POWER OF PRAISE

We must dismiss those who say that praise is powerless. That anyone who believes the Bible could ever make such a claim is astonishing. Out of scores of possible references, consider just two, Nehemiah 8:10, "The joy of the Lord is your strength!" *and Psalm 22:3,* "God is enthroned upon the praises of his people."

The latter passage reflects the idea that when a king desires to speak with authority or to exercise royal power, he first sits upon his throne. When he speaks from the throne, clothed with majesty, his regal command brooks no denial. The psalmist thinks of God in the same way. He is saying: if you want God to act for you in awesome power, if you want to see his royal hand stretched out to work on your behalf, then set up for him a throne. From that throne he will speak as a King should speak; he will do as a King should do. His promise and his power will both be yours. You may ask: "How can I set up his throne?" *The psalmist answers:* "Build a throne of praise. God enthrones himself upon the praises of his people!"

But the contrary notion, that praise is all-powerful, and especially the idea that you should praise God for everything, no matter what happens, is nearly as bad -

THE LIMITS OF PRAISE

How can I praise God for what Satan and sin do? Is there no room for tears, for sorrow, for pain? Praising God for everything that happens to us, whether good or bad, is the same as calling God the source of all those things. Yet the Bible forbids us to attribute to God things that arise from corrupt flesh or from Satan (cp. James 1:13). Praising God for everything also forces a sorrowing heart into an unnatural response. Sometimes it is more appropriate to weep than to laugh; a sigh will then be more human than a song, and a prayer will come more readily than praise (James 5:13; Ecclesiastes 3:4; Proverbs 14:10, 13, 13:12). To deny people the right to mourn, or to express bitterness of heart, or to grieve in the presence of injustice, savagery, tragedy, and the like, is to deprive them of part of their God-given humanity. Remember, the Bible contains almost as many Psalms of lament as it does Hymns of praise. Sometimes the most honest thing to do in the presence of God is to declare your anger, frustration, or grief.

So a better view is to hold that praise is indeed powerful, but not all-powerful; and that while I cannot praise God for everything I can certainly praise him in everything. That is, no matter how dark the night may be, there is always some comfort, some grace, some gift of God to be found, and for that I can praise him - like the poet, who found no joy in the valley of the shadow of death itself, but rather for the comfort his Shepherd gave him (Psalm 23:4).

Similarly, we Christians may find, and thank God for, comfort in sorrow, enabling grace in trial, an upholding arm in weakness, inner joy in the midst of tears, a name still written in heaven despite our failures; and so on. The principle is, even in the blackest hour there is always something for which to praise the Lord - a song to sing (Job 35:10; Psalm 42:8; 77:6), a joy to tell, a salvation to grasp with gladness.

Would you not think it unnatural, absurd, if not actually ungodly, to rejoice because the night has enveloped you? But in the midst of the darkness, and despite it, the trusting heart can always find some gift of God, precious, powerful, for which to praise him. That praise then becomes a strong step toward deliverance, or toward God's eventual answer to your prayer (cp. 2 Corinthians 1:3-5; etc.)

In the remainder of this study I want to use Israel as an example of the quality of praise God requires of us. Notice first that

ISRAEL WAS A PRAISING NATION

The quality of praise God demanded from Israel was remarkable. There was nothing sedate or ornately dignified about it. The people were expected to be exuberant, excited, joyful, spontaneous, and tireless in their praise. They were to dance, and sing, and celebrate, not just for a minute or two, but for hours at a time, and sometimes for days!

> *"The Levites and priests sang to the Lord every day, accompanied by the Lord's instruments of praise ... For seven days they praised the Lord... The whole assembly agreed to celebrate the festival seven more days; so for another seven days they celebrated joyfully!"*[30]

> *" ... with all their heart and soul ... with loud acclamation, with shouting, and with trumpets and horns, all Judah rejoiced ... They sought God eagerly, and he was found by them."*[31]

Similar references are scattered through the Old Testament, plus scores of references in the Psalms, such as -

> *"Shout with joy to God, all the earth! Sing to the glory of his name! Offer him glory and praise ... Praise our God, O peoples, let the sound of his praise be heard ... I cried out to him with my mouth, his praise was on my tongue!"*[32]

Israel's prosperity, military success, conquest of her enemies, possession of the Promised Land, were all substantially contingent upon the quality of her praise. Poor praise led to defeat and dispossession; good praise brought heaven's bounty. When the people of Israel praised God with all their heart they became invincible; no foe could stand before them; victory and prosperity were assured: 2 Chronicles 13:14-15; 20:22-23; Judges 7:20-22; Joshua 6:20; Psalm 103:1-5; 30:1-4. No wonder there are more than 500 references in the Bible to the necessity and joy of praising God!

Christian Jews in the early church remembered that principle well. Thus praise brought Paul and Silas out of prison (Acts 16:25-26). Will praise always produce such a dramatic result? Of course not, otherwise there would never have been any martyrs in the history of the church. But true praise will bring change into any situation - if not releasing you from it, at least giving you strength to overcome it

---

[30] 2 Ch 30:21-23.

[31] 2 Ch 15:12-15.

[32] 66:1-2,8,17 and also 68:3-4; 28:7-8; 149:2-9.

(2 Corinthians 12:7-10). Praise enables God to bring a redemptive grace into your life from even the most wretched events.

How hard it would be, nay ridiculous, to apply such descriptions to the kind of praise that is heard in countless churches in our day. How monotonous, how dreary, how routine, how passionless, is the sound of their worship! Where is the gladness, the exultation, the zeal, the happy, almost riotous clamor of a people excited at being welcomed by the God of all heaven and earth? What stern rebuke would the saints of old give us if they could hear the mechanical mumbles that we often hear droned in the presence of the King!

Israel again gives us an example, but this time of the consequences of inadequate praise. Despite their songs, the people were overrun by their enemies, ruin and slavery fell upon them, sickness and poverty overwhelmed them. Why? Because not all praise deserves the name ...

THE MARKS OF FALSE PRAISE

Read Jeremiah 7:1-11. Jeremiah was told to go into the temple when it was thronged with worshippers, and to denounce their worship. What was wrong? God declined to accept the worship of the people, because their praise was

MAGICAL, NOT SPIRITUAL

Note the repeated rebuke,

> *"You trust in deceptive words! ... You trust in deceptive words!"* (verses 4 & 8).

The meaning is, they had reduced praise to a superstitious formula, as though the mere mouthing of words would attract the power of God. Thus they were copying the pagan practices of their idolatrous neighbors, who firmly believed that using the correct incantation could compel the gods to do the will of man. From this belief the priests and wizards gained their power, for they alone were in possession of the most secret spells, the most magic formulae. But everyone in that ancient world knew at least some chants that could charm the gods into subservience and make them obedient slaves of the spell-casters. Just repeat the magic words over and over, and lo, the miracle is done!

But such notions were hateful to God. Mere words, divorced from true worship, were worthless mockery. No words, standing alone, have any power to influence the Lord, except perhaps to arouse his anger! *Words* of praise move heaven only when they are pouring tumultuously out of a *heart* of praise. Apart from warm love, genuine gratitude, fervent adoration, praise becomes nothing more than a clattering cacophony (1 Corinthians 13:1).

Yet there are those who imagine if only they can find the right way to say the right words, the mere saying of those words will guarantee an answer from heaven. Conversely, they also suppose that any mistake in what they say will at once rob them of the promised blessing. But that brings praise into the realm of superstition, not faith. Any attempt to reduce praise to a formula, to make success dependent upon a certain prescription, apart from genuine faith and heartfelt worship, turns prayer into a pagan ritual, empty of spiritual vitality. Do not suppose that just because you say, *"Praise God"*, or speak the name of *"Jesus"*, or shout, *"Hallelujah!"* that such words (if they are only words) have any power over God? They do not, unless they are warmly and sincerely spoken, in a setting of loving trust and true gladness in God.

So guard against the delusion that you can oblige God to do your will just because you have spoken certain words in his presence. That is magical superstition, not faith.

Then false praise often has this character; it is

HYPOCRITICAL, NOT HOLY

See verses 9-11. Notice the Lord's indignation -

> *"Will you steal and murder, and then come into my House and say, `We are safe'? You will never be safe if you go on doing all these detestable things!"*

The scene is this: the Babylonians were threatening to overrun Palestine, but the people were convinced they had found a way to fend off the invader - they would praise God in his holy temple. When they had done this, they declared themselves safe. But God refused to allow them safety if they intended to continue in their wicked lifestyle. The sword of Babylon would run them through right there in the house of God while they were chanting their hypocritical anthems.

They were like people today who think they can maintain two lifestyles: one inside the church and another outside. But God cannot permit us to remain unscathed if we try at the same time to hold a double identity, godly and ungodly. Two levels of spirituality, one that you present to God and one that you present to the world, are not acceptable. It is all or nothing with our God. He demands total commitment. Which means you should be the same outside the church as you are in it, the same in private as you are in public - showing the same face, displaying the same demeanor, saying the same words.

God measures the validity of the praise we offer him inside the church by the quality and constancy of the praise we offer him outside the church. In other words, a given moment of praise is effective only when it is part of a whole life committed to praise. This does not mean that praise becomes effective only after so many weeks or months, but rather that praise does not become effective at all unless the believer has made a commitment to praise God for ever!

None of us, of course, maintains perfect constancy in praise. The best of us often forget and fall short of the song we want to sing. But that does not destroy the value of our praise, providing we remain firm in our commitment to live for God and to praise him for ever.

ROUTINE, NOT CREATIVE

Note the three-fold,

> *"This is the temple of the Lord, this is the temple of the Lord, this is the temple of the Lord!"*

It shows that their praise had become a mindless routine, an empty ritual, a repetitious mouthing of religious cliches, monotonous, mechanical, utterly tedious to God. He refused to listen to it. It lacked both heart and mind; they gave no thought to their praise, it had no feeling to inflame it.

Be warned! Praise that has lapsed into a hollow habit is not welcome by God. In a score of places scripture urges us to put thought and feeling into worship. Sing a new song! Find a new way to magnify the Lord! Be creative, innovative, different, alive, in your thanksgiving! Arouse yourself from apathy! Banish boredom! Cast aside carelessness! True praise demands the best from you, body, mind, and spirit! See Psalm 33:3; 40:3; 96:1; 98:1; 144:9; 149:1; Isaiah 42:10.

You may not be a poet, nor do you have to be. If you love the Lord with passion, if he is more than life to you, if his joy is your strength and happiness, you will not lack wonderful words to tell him so! So give attention to what you are saying in worship, prayer, and praise, and strive for new words to express your love and gratitude to God. It is hardly enough just to keep on saying "praise the Lord", or "hallelujah", or "glory to God", or some other stock phrase, over and over and over again. That is just mindless repetition (Matthew 6:7). If you cannot think of anything different, use the scriptures. The Psalms are full of wonderful ideas for praise!

CEREMONIAL, NOT PROPHETIC

See 1 Corinthians 14:23-25. Notice just one thing: when the church at Corinth met for worship, and *"they all prophesied,"* growth irresistibly occurred. Unbelievers and outsiders found themselves drawn to that place, brought under conviction of sin, and soon joined the company of worshipping believers.

What does it mean, *"they all prophesied"*? Probably several things, but among them at least this: there was a prophetic quality about all their worship. From the opening greeting to the closing benediction a mantle of prophecy rested upon their ministry, whether to each other or to God. That is what made their worship so powerful. Interwoven with the sound of the human voices there was a divine accent.

A service that was little more than formal ceremony, or fixed routine, was not acceptable to that Spirit-filled worshipping community. They demanded a manifestation of divine life. They were content with nothing less than the presence of God. They depended upon the inspiration of the Holy Spirit. They wanted to hear God's voice more than man's.

What would they have thought of a worship service where the sound of revelry was heard in place of the sound of prophecy, or where ritual was more important than revelation, or formality more revered than freedom?

You may ask: "What about a formal liturgy, repeated verbatim each Sunday?"

Plainly, the scriptures leave ample room for such a worship-style (compare the highly structured worship of ancient Israel, and the Psalms, which rightly became repeated litanies in the temple). But if worship never steps outside the set pattern, or if the liturgy leaves no room for free and spontaneous expression, then the praises of the people will almost certainly decay into a lifeless routine. Place must be found for us, as it was also for Israel, both inside the church and outside of it, to express in our own words and way, the joy of Christ.

Dignity and order have a necessary place in good worship (1 Corinthians 14:40); but they are no substitute for bringing the church to the place where, when the people come together and begin to praise God, behold, *"they all prophesy"!*

How can we create this quality of *prophetic* worship? That is not an easy question to answer; but certain things are obvious: (a) consciously set the goal of creating prophetic worship; (b) saturate the service with prayer; (c) let nothing disturb the unity of the church; (d) stir up the faith of the people; and the like.

As an example of prophetic praise, consider the Psalms. They show how prophetic Israel's praise was at its best. And what power that praise has had through the Psalms, and still has! There is no better demonstration of praise upon which the mantle of prophecy rests. Yet how much more effective, how much more anointed, should the worship of Spirit-filled believers be! And that is the picture Paul gives in 1 Corinthians 14, of the church coming together as a worshipping community, of the spirit of prophecy permeating all their praise and ministry, of outsiders being drawn to them, of sinners being converted, of supernatural gifts flourishing, of the church irresistibly growing. If we can develop in our churches the same kind of spiritual, holy, creative, and prophetic praise, we will see the same astonishing result!

CONCLUSION

The existence of spurious praise alongside genuine praise arises from the fact that only the lively can truly praise God; the dead cannot praise him (as the following references show by a metaphor, Psalm 6:5; 88:10; 115:17; Isaiah 38:18-19.)

Where spiritual *death* prevails, praise always becomes magical, hypocritical, routine, and ceremonial.

But spiritual *life* reveals itself in praise that is *spiritual, holy, creative, and prophetic*.

POINTS TO PONDER

(1) What is wrong with the idea that we should praise God for everything that happens?

(2) What is the significance of the idea that "God is enthroned upon the praises of his people"?

(3) Think of some bleak situations in life, times of crisis, or sorrow. What are some of the things you could praise God for in those times?

(4) What effect did true praise have in Israel's history?

(5) How do Christians change praise into a magical formula?

(6) For it to be truly effective, what environment must praise occur in?

(7) How can you ensure that your praise is "creative", that you are obeying the biblical injunction to sing to God a "new" song?

(8) What should a congregation do to keep a prophetic quality in its praise?

NO SWEAT!

> *"They must wear linen turbans upon their heads, and linen breeches upon their loins; they must not gird themselves with anything that causes sweat."*[33]

The prophet Ezekiel saw a vision of the great temple of God, and his description of what he saw gives us a picture of the splendor of the coming kingdom of God, the heavenly Jerusalem. Some people think the temple will one day be built, just as Ezekiel described it; but that seems improbable. Many of the details he provided - such as the changed topography of the land, the restoration of animal sacrifices, the peculiar dimensions of the City - are contrary both to nature and the gospel. It is better to read a spiritual or figurative sense into the vision than a literal one.

Among the mass of instructions about the temple, given in the last eight chapters of his prophecy, is the one found in our text. Ezekiel said that the priests in the holy temple of God were forbidden to gird themselves with anything that causes sweat. *What does that mean? Apparently this: God does not want "sweaty" service from any of his servants. You do not need to, nor can you, "sweat" your way into the kingdom of God. You get there by the grace of God or you don't get there at all! If there is any toil and labor to be done, the Lord will do it. The labor that brings us to the heavenly altar has already been completed by Jesus, in the garden of Gethsemane and on the cross. God does not want, nor will he accept, any "sweaty" service from us.*

From this symbolic rule - "they shall not gird themselves with anything that causes sweat" - *we can learn some important lessons about grace.*

YOU CAN'T SWEAT YOUR WAY TO A NEW POSITION.

What is the thing we hunger most to gain from God? Surely it is the splendid prize of having uncluttered access to the throne of God, of being able to hold our heads up, of freedom to be bold in the presence of our God. What boon equals the right to approach the Lord without any sense of a barrier between us and our King? How sweet to know that no gulf lies between us and heaven that has to be bridged! This is the poignant longing the psalmist expressed -

---

[33] Ez 44:18.

> *"How passionately I love your dwelling place, O Lord Almighty. My heart yearns, it faints with longing, to walk in the courts of the Lord. Everything within me cries earnestly for you, the living God."*[34]

He was thinking about more than the temple in Jerusalem when he sang those wistful words. His heart was reaching toward the heavenly throne of God, the spiritual altar, and he echoed the yearning that is in the soul of every believer. How we long to come into that sweet place, into the dwelling-place of God, to stand before the King of all heaven and earth, and there to worship him! We crave the joy of kneeling at the throne with the angels, those holy seraphim and cherubim. Oh! that like them we might be privileged never to leave the presence of the Majesty of heaven.

But whenever we approach the Lord we find that our sin is a barrier between us and God. Whenever we try to step into the Father's presence, at once an awareness of our wrong-doing arises before us. Our corrupt and fallen condition creates an uncrossable hiatus between us and the Holy One. We feel driven to cry out, *"How can I, unclean as I am, come into the presence of the Lord?"* We feel that if our eyes were ever privileged to see God, it would in fact be our undoing.

We are like the prophet Isaiah, when he saw the glory of the Lord in the temple in Jerusalem, and cried,

> *"Woe to me! I am ruined! I am a man of unclean lips, and I live among a people of unclean lips, yet my eyes have seen the King, the Lord God Almighty."* [35]

Our immediate instinct is to solve this problem by a frenzy of good works. We say to ourselves, "Surely if I work at it I can get into God's presence. Surely if I accumulate enough good deeds, if I make enough sacrifices, or just give more money, more time, more effort, I will be able to work my way into the presence of God."

But that is the very thing the prophet countermands by his stern injunction, "The priests shall not gird themselves with anything that causes sweat."

He means simply, there is no way, by any effort of ours, that we can earn a place before the altar of God. There is no way we can ever deserve it by doing good works. Does that mean we shouldn't do good things, we shouldn't busy ourselves with righteous activities, or we shouldn't make whatever sacrifices are

---

[34] Ps 84:1-2

[35] Is 6:5

called from us by the Lord? Of course not. We are plainly told to occupy ourselves with good works until Jesus comes. We are commanded to take up our cross and follow Jesus, and to be diligent in the service of our King, day and night, all the days of our lives. But that should all be a consequence of trusting the grace of God, not a means of trying to merit that grace. We serve the Lord because we are already standing in his presence, not because we are trying to get there.

When it comes to this matter of our spiritual standing before the Lord, we cannot sweat our way into a new position. There is nothing you and I can do that will make us more deserving of having our prayers answered today than we were yesterday. At least, there is nothing we can do except trust in the grace of God. By his grace and gift alone we gain all the merit we shall ever need to have our prayers answered.

So never imagine that you can double God's willingness to answer prayer by doubling your tithes and offerings to the church, or doubling your pious deeds. It doesn't work that way. You can't go to church on Sunday morning and say, "Hey, I need God to do something bigger and better this week, so I'm going to give twice as much today as I gave last week." *As though you can buy your way into God's presence; as though you can put God under pressure because of what you have done; as though he is more moved by your works than he is by the work of Christ.* No, says God, "In my holy house, I will do the sweating; you will just do the getting!"

What does that mean to us? First, we should have a yearning like the psalmist had, to be in the presence of the Lord, to walk in his splendid courts, to have our eyes open to behold the beauty of the Lord and to joy in him, in his presence, his love, his grace. But then, second, we must recognize that there is only one way to attain that grace of God: by receiving it as his gift in Jesus.

> **Into thy presence I come,**
> **not by the works I have done,**
> **but by thy grace**
> **and thy grace alone,**
> **into thy presence I come."**

Not God's grace plus what you add to it, but by his grace alone.

What is his grace? Is it just his kindness toward us? Just his undeserved love toward you and me? It is that, but also much more. It is his eager desire to reach out to us because of what Christ has done for us, to catch us up and to bring us into his presence, to surround us with his love, and by his own gift to make us deserving of the very best he can do. To obtain all those things we need do no more than sing the refrain of faith. Let the Spirit of God plant the theme into your innermost heart, "Lord, nothing in my hand I bring, simply to thy cross I cling."

David once said he would not come into the presence of God with an offering that cost him nothing[36]. No doubt there are times when that remains a proper attitude. But not when you want access to the throne of God, not when you are seeking the right to stand in God's presence enjoying uncluttered communion with him, able to claim every blessing that resides in his promise. In that case you had better come empty-handed, depending only upon his grace.

Paul expressed the same idea beautifully in his letter to the Galatians -

> *"You know that no one can be justified by observing the law, but only by faith in Jesus Christ. Even we apostles must put our faith in Christ Jesus, so that we may be justified by faith in Christ and not by keeping some law, because no one will be justified by obeying the requirements of the law."*[37]

When Paul talks about *"the works of the law"* he means any good work, or sacrifice, or rule, that you impose upon yourself, thinking it will give you some special access to God, some special right to come into the Father's presence or to approach him in prayer. No, says Paul, we believe in Jesus Christ so that we can approach God in prayer. We believe in Jesus Christ so that we abandon all hope of building righteousness by obeying the dictates of the law. Jesus himself is the door, and we need no other. The law is banished as a means of buying the favor of God. You cannot sweat your way into a new position in the heavenlies!

YOU CAN'T SWEAT YOUR WAY TO A NEW PROSPERITY

I have encountered a strange idea among some Christians; a peculiar argument that runs like this: if an ungodly person can go out into the world and make a million dollars, I, being a child of God, can surely go out and make two million dollars. If the ungodly can have it, I can have more of it. If the ungodly can do it, I can do more of it."

So there are Christian people who, in the name of Christ, work furiously, trying to build a prosperity that will make the ungodly ashamed.

No doubt there *are* some people whom God calls, and gives the opportunity, the giftings, the skills, to go out and to amass great wealth. The Lord intends, of course, that they should then pour their riches back into the kingdom of God,

---

[36] 2 Sa 24:24
[37] Ga 2:26

clothing the naked, housing the homeless, feeding the hungry, building the church, and the like.

However, it is equally sure that the of gathering of wealth does not lie in the call of God for most of his servants. Therefore, we need to be careful about how we understand the term "prosperity", and what that term means to those who are in the kingdom of God.

Let me show you something the Bible says about the ungodly, which many Christians fail to understand: *God will not let his children do what he lets the unrighteous do.* He doesn't much care about the actions of the unrighteous; whatever they do is damning them anyway, digging a straight tunnel to hell. But when he deals with his own children, the Lord keeps them from doing whatever they want; he does not easily allow them to disregard his program for their life. This rule applies to getting rich.

Look what the Lord says about the ungodly. The idea I have in mind occurs in many places in scripture, but some verses from Proverbs will suffice:

>**Proverbs 10:16**, "The wages of the righteous bring them life, but the income of the wicked brings them punishment."

Mark that. Solomon is talking about the wealth, the prosperity, the luxury, the success that the wicked pile around themselves, things that often create envy in the hearts of the righteous (and may they blush with shame for that envy.) But all the time they fail to understand that this very wealth, as often as not, is the very judgment of God upon the wicked. It is a destruction from the Almighty. He allows them to gather their millions as an expression of his anger against them. They reap the doom that heaven's righteousness has pronounced on them in their greed, their selfishness, their carnality, their worldliness, their rebellion against God, their failure to seek the real purpose of God for their lives. God judges from the heavens, and he says, *"Since you choose to walk against my will, and to heap up riches, I will give you still more wealth, and it will damn your soul!"* Their very gain is their doom.

Now don't misunderstand me. I am not saying that every rich person is damned, or that there is anything intrinsically wrong in wealth. God may give great wealth to his own children as a sign of his blessing and favor and as part of his purpose for their lives. I am not talking against riches as such, but rather about the person who obeys God versus the person who does not. For the person who is disobeying God, wealth is not a blessing, wealth is a double damnation to his soul.

>**Proverbs 15:6.** "In the home of the righteous you will find great riches; but the treasure of the wicked brings them nothing but trouble."

The wicked make money their god; they amass it by millions, by hundreds of millions, even thousands of millions. But trouble befalls the income of the wicked.

I have been in poor homes where there was endless happiness, and I have been in rich homes were there was endless misery. I have also been in poor homes where there was endless misery, and in rich homes where there was endless happiness. What does it mean? It means that neither wealth nor poverty is anything, but obedience to God is everything. It means that righteousness alone is real wealth, and submission to the will and purpose of God for your life, whatever that might mean - whether a vast bank balance, or no bank balance at all. Submission to the will of God is the only thing that has real significance in human life.

Proverbs 23:4. "Why do you wear yourself out just to get rich? Be wise enough to show restraint. Turn your eye away from your money for only a moment, and suddenly it is gone! It sprouts wings and flies out of sight like an eagle in the sky!"

Does that mean the righteous can never be rich? No, but it means you ought not to toil just to be rich. If God wants you to be rich, you will gather wealth without sweating for it. And if God does not want you rich, no matter how much you sweat, it will bring you no wealth. It might bring you money, but it won't bring you wealth. With all your money, you will be cramped and miserable and mean in your spirit. You will be a sorry, wretched specimen of broken humanity. If you have to sweat to get wealth, then desist, says the wise man. While there is still time to save your soul, take a different path. Have the wisdom to back off and relax!

Jesus meant it when he said, *"My yoke is easy, and my burden is light."* [38]No Christian should emulate the sweating, frenzied, bothered, bewitched, burdened ways of this world. Leave it to the world to worry it's way to hell. Why should the saints of light copy that madness?

I am not advising you just to sit home, do nothing, and say, *"Well, here I am God, drop some golden coins on me."* No, for of course we are called to work. God requires us to be diligent. Scripture contains many warnings about the sorry fate of the slothful, the foolish, the stupid. It has little patience with those who fail to plan or to prepare for tomorrow.

> *"Go to the ant, you sluggard; consider its ways and be wise!"* [39]

---

[38] Mt 11:30

[39] Pr 6:6-11

Look around you; see how God, everywhere in his universe, gives examples that show how food and housing, comfort and well-being, go to the diligent. Happiness and prosperity come to those who plan, who seek counsel, who allow the wisdom of God to guide and motivate their lives.

But for all that, there is a difference between diligent labor in obedience to God's program for your life, and the kind of sweaty, anxious, struggling, troubled toil of this world. We need to learn that difference.

A pastor, for example, can put together many programs, and work, work, work to build his congregation bigger and bigger. He can toil and labor, and burn himself out before he is half through his expected years of ministry, and think he has done God a great service. How proud he is of his vast congregation! Yet he has done nothing except gather a crowd. He differs little from the millionaire who gloats over his amassed gold. Collecting a congregation and building a church are not the same thing. A large audience does not make a church! That crowd of people will become a church only when they are bonded together in love under the full lordship of Christ. A church is more than people coming together for a religious ceremony, a sacred performance, once a week.

I am not saying that either small or large churches are better than each other, but that a group of people become a church only when they enter into a covenant relationship with each other in Christ. More importantly, no preacher has to "sweat" to build the church God wants him to build. He should simply put on the easy yoke of the Lord as he takes up the light burden of the dream the Lord has given him.

The same is true for every Christian, no matter what your role in life. We must all take up the burden of the Lord; but his yoke is *easy and his burden* is *light*. *If you are frenzied, pressured, anxious, troubled, pressed, bothered and bewildered, then you need to back off and take another look at yourself and your affairs. Say, "Lord, where have I gone wrong?" Get your life back into divine order. If you are God's servant you will not gird yourself with anything that makes you "sweat". If you are "sweating", then you had better ungird yourself. God's turban is linen and God's gown is linen. It is cool, white, and easy to wear!*

So you can't sweat your way to a new position, and you can't sweat your way to a new prosperity. It is also true that

YOU CAN'T SWEAT YOUR WAY TO A NEW POWER

As I write these words I know that my own ears need to hear this message. I am as much inclined as anyone to do the things I am condemning! All too easily I allow the flesh, the world, even the church to gird me with things that will make me "sweat". Especially here, for we are all prone to "sweat" our way to a new power, with God, over the works of the devil, and over the kingdom of darkness.

Perhaps you are grappling with sin; or maybe sickness is attacking your health and happiness; or somehow the devil and his minions are threatening your life and seeking to destroy you? You know that in Jesus' name we are supposed to rise up in the power of God and drive back the forces of darkness. So at once we say to ourselves, "I don't have enough power, I've got to get more. I need power to work miracles, to drive back sin, to heal the sick, to cast out demons. How can I get more power?" *Then we get all sweaty over it. We grit our teeth,* "I'll fast, I'll pray; somehow I will break through to power with God!"

God knows I've gone through that routine often enough. And the Spirit of God has come back to me, admonished me and said, "Son, don't you remember reading there in the scripture, `You must not gird yourself with anything that makes you sweat? When you come into my presence you must come before me cool and easy, for I will not accept a sweaty priest!"

Jesus put his finger on it beautifully in the gospel of Luke 10:18-19. He said to them,

> *"I saw Satan falling like lightning from heaven, and I have given you authority to trample on snakes and scorpions and to overcome all the power of the enemy, so that nothing can harm you."*

Notice two words Jesus used there. He said, "I give you <u>authority</u> over the <u>power</u> of the enemy," which in this case is also a close translation of the original Greek text of Luke. The contrast is between authority and power. "Power" is a thing of sweat and toil, but "authority" is not. The one who has authority and knows it always has the advantage over one who has mere power.

Here is an illustration of what I mean. In March 1815 Napoleon Bonaparte escaped from the island of Elba, where he had been imprisoned by the Allied Powers after the defeat of the French armies. From the time of his escape he had 100 days of freedom, culminating in the great Battle of Waterloo. There Napoleon was finally crushed by the British general, the Duke of Wellington.

Before then, shortly after he had landed on the shores of France with a handful of friends, Napoleon had a remarkable encounter with a body of French soldiers who were coming to arrest him. Panic had gripped Paris when word of Napoleon's escape reached the city, and the king had sent a large contingent of troops to the coast, with orders to stop him or kill him.

When Napoleon saw the army he told his friends to stand back while he walked on alone. He was a little man, hardly more than 5 feet tall. But he went boldly along the road toward the host of soldiers. When he got within sound of them he unbuttoned his coat, tore it open, presented his chest as a target, and then cried, "Soldiers of France, would you shoot your emperor?"

Immediately the soldiers threw down their muskets and began to shout, and cheer, and hurrah. In a moment they were all behind Napoleon as he marched on triumphantly to Paris.

That is an example of authority against power. The soldiers had no authority; all they had was power. They had muskets, powder, balls and other weapons of war; but that is all they had - power. Napoleon had no power, not even a pistol on his hip. But he had authority and knew it. As always, authority was tougher than power!

But suppose Napoleon had stood before those soldiers all buttoned up, and trembling, and said in a piteous, pleading voice, "Men, I was a prisoner of the British on Elba; but I've managed to escape, and now I am standing here on this dusty road, wholly at your mercy. Please don't shoot me." *The likelihood is, he would soon have been a corpse riddled with bullets. He was not so pusillanimous. He declared,* "I stand here as your Emperor!" *He took authority, and an army knelt in the dust before one small man and gave him homage.*

That is what Jesus meant when he said, "I give you authority over all the power of the enemy." You see, the devil has no authority; he only has power, and he has lots of it. He has more power than you will ever have. You can pray for power until you perish, but you will never have anything that remotely compares to the power the enemy holds. He has power beyond our imagination. All the weapons of all the nations of this world are as pebbles compared to the sheer energy Satan has available to him.

Should we then cower before the Prince of Darkness? Hardly! He may have power, but what is that against authority? We possess the authority of Christ himself, which he said is immensely greater than all the power of the enemy!

So you don't need to feel strong when you're confronting the devil. It matters nothing whether you feel strong or not. You don't have to feel that you have the power of God crackling in your fingers when you come against Satan. You need only know who you are in Christ, so that you can proclaim, "Satan I am your Emperor!"

Shed a tear for the devil, who must sweat hard for everything he does. He has to sweat it out, and he is sweating it out. He has nothing else to depend upon. His only method is sweat, power, toil, work, and worry. In Satan's realm of lies, deceit, and darkness, there is only anxiety and trouble!.

Over all the demons of hell the authority we have in Christ is supreme. Yet that authority is not something you can work for, it is not something you deserve, nor can you sweat to get it. Jesus said, "I give you authority." *We are left with no choice except to take up gratefully this God-given authority, rejoicing in that great kindness the Father has shown us in Christ. The greatest thing you can discover is who you are in Christ, and what belongs to you in his name without any sweat on your part.*

In the middle of the last century Sir Charles Simpson became one of the great benefactors of mankind when he discovered chloroform. At last a way was found to rid men and women of the scourge of pain. However, it was several years before his discovery was accepted. The medical world was suspicious of such a radical departure from past practice, and the religious world also opposed the use of chloroform, especially in child birth - many of the clergy argued that it was the will of God for women to suffer in childbirth. Sir Charles Simpson was an obstetrician, and he was deeply concerned about alleviating the pain of the women he attended, which heightened the resentment he encountered. So his discovery was largely ignored, until Queen Victoria used chloroform in the birth of Prince Leopold. Almost at once, anesthesia was universally accepted - the Queen's endorsement was too influential to resist!

Many years later, toward the end of his life, a journalist came to Sir Charles and said to him, "Across a lifetime of scientific endeavor, what would you say is the greatest discovery you have made?" *Of course, the journalist expected Sir Charles to select out of the many achievements of his long and fruitful life the discovery of chloroform, that miraculous gift to mankind.*

But without a moment's hesitation, the great physician looked at the journalist and said simply and humbly, "The finest discovery I ever made was the discovery that Jesus Christ is my Saviour."

There was a wise man! Nothing can surpass the discovery of Jesus and all the authority that he represents: authority over sin, authority over sickness, authority over fear, authority over all the powers of darkness. Yet there is nothing for us to do to make that discovery except to have the heart to see it and believe it and take it as God's gift in Christ. Then step out in Jesus' name and use that authority to overcome the enemy and to fulfil the purpose of God.

Let the Holy Spirit burn these words into your soul. When you come into the presence of your God, to offer him service, to be obedient to his will, to seize all that is yours in Christ, act on this principle: you must not gird yourself with anything that makes you sweat. *Be content with God's grace. Clothe yourself with the snowy-white cool linen of his righteousness. Approach the throne with confidence and joy, by faith grasping everything that belongs to you in salvation, healing, prosperity, and victory. Why sweat when you don't have to?*

POINTS TO PONDER

(1) What is the greatest boon we desire from God? What is the most common barrier to obtaining that boon?

(2) How do we gain full access to the throne of God? Is there anything we can do for ourselves that will increase our right to approach the throne?

(3) What place do good works have in a Christian's life? Do they have any *value or use?*

(4) What did Paul mean by his reference to "works of the law"? Was he thinking only about the laws of Moses, or did he include other things?

(5) When ungodly people amass great wealth, should this be seen as a sign of divine favour, or of divine judgment? Can riches actually be a mark of judgment rather than of blessing?

(6) In relation to our spiritual welfare, which is the preferable state: wealth, or poverty?

(7) What difference does this chapter draw between working diligently (which we should all do), and "sweating" to achieve a goal?

(8) Look at your own life. Can you honestly say there is no place where you are "sweating" either to achieve something for *God, or to gain something* from *him?*

(9) Do you agree that "one who has authority and knows it always has the advantage over one who has mere power"?

(10) What is the spiritual significance to us of "girding ourselves with linen turbans and linen breeches"?

MUCH, MUCH MORE!

> *"If that were not enough, I would have given you much, much more"* (2 Samuel 12:8).

Nathan's prophecy shows that David could have, and should have, made himself the ruler of the greatest empire the world had ever seen. He should have established his dominion over Egypt, Mesopotamia, Canaan, perhaps even Persia, and many other lands. A promise of world empire lies in that phrase, *"much, much more"*. God had given David much, but he was willing to give him *more, much more,* **much, much more!**

David should have committed himself to the task of bringing the law and the name of the living God to every nation within reach of his armies.

How can I be sure of that? Because -

    a. That was the commission God had already given Israel.[40] Their task was to carry his laws and his righteousness to the ends of the earth. In that ancient time, the only way to accomplish this missionary purpose of God was by forcing the nations one by one to join the commonwealth of Israel.

    b. God had promised to make them the chief of the nations and to give them the wealth of the heathen[41] Despite the great success David had enjoyed, Israel was still a small and poor nation. Vast portions of the incredible promises God had given to their fathers still remained unfulfilled, waiting for a man of faith to embrace and bring into reality.

    c. The Lord himself had actually *commanded* David to ask for and possess a world-wide empire.[42] How far short of that goal he still remained!

    d. God gave that inheritance, and more, to many heathen kings, who showed more zeal for their dead gods than any of the kings of Israel were able to muster for the living God. Consequently, the peoples of the earth were

---

[40] See Is 43:11-13

[41] De:12,13; Leviticus 26:7,8.

[42] Ps2:8 There is of course a reference on this Psalm to Christ, and it will find its greatest fulfillment in him. Nonetheless, the original promise, or better, command was to David.

compelled to worship the gods of Egypt, Babylon, Assyria, Greece, or Rome, instead of being drawn to worship the Lord God of Israel. Even the covenant people began to wonder at times if those heathen gods were not more powerful than their Lord. Yet whose fault was it? The empires that God gave to Sennacherib the Assyrian, or to Nebuchadnezzar the Babylonian, or to Cyrus the Persian, do you not think he would rather have given to one of his own sons? But the Lord could not find a godly man with the heart to possess the promise. So the nations continued to groan under a burden of tyranny and idolatry, when they could have rejoiced under the just laws and covenant of the living God.

> ***e.*** The principle of the kingdom of God is increase - *"of the increase of his government ... upon the throne of David, and over his kingdom ... there shall be no end."* [43] Therefore, whatever is in harmony with that kingdom will be in a state of increase. Where increase is no longer observed, the kingdom is no longer functioning as it should be.

If God was so eager to give David *"much, much more"*, why did the king fail to obtain it?

If you are familiar with the story of David, you will probably say, "Obviously, because of his dreadful crime against Uriah!" But that crime was not so much the *cause* of David's loss as it was a *symptom* of a deeper spiritual malaise. His real failure had its roots in a spiritual decay that took place long before he took Bathsheba into his bed.

I can see at least three parts to David's spiritual collapse -

HE SET BOUNDARIES WHERE GOD HAD NOT SET THEM

The story suggests that David had lost his ambition to expand the borders of Israel. What could have caused that dullness?

Perhaps he had reached a point where he was satisfied with his kingdom and his possessions. So he stopped wanting what God wanted him to possess. Israel, in fact, never did fully *"possess their possessions"*[44]. But if a servant of God ever stops wanting *all* that God has made available to him, he will begin to want what God has not made available to him. So David, losing his hunger for Israel's increase, began to lust instead for another man's wife.

---

[43] Is 9:7.
[44] Ob 17.

Perhaps he found the promise of God too big to believe. Perhaps his faith could encompass *"the house of Judah and the house of Israel, and the throne of Saul"* - but to believe also for the thrones of Egypt, Babylon, Syria, and so on - that was too much!

Perhaps he let the enemies of Israel, rather than the promise of God, set the boundaries of the nation.

All three of those faults are still common among God's people:

- there are those who say "enough" long before God has said "enough"; they are content with a little when God wants to give them much.

- there are those who simply stagger before God's promises, who are paralysed by unbelief, who refuse to stir themselves to believe and to receive all that God has planned for them.

- there are those who allow the world, the devil, the flesh, to forge the perimeters of their lives, who refuse to make the effort to break loose from those chains.

But the command of scripture is clear. If you want to be in harmony with the kingdom of God, then you must be committed to *increase* - today, tomorrow, and forever! Increase in every aspect of your life and Christian service. Increase in all that you receive from the hand of the Lord. Increase in your faith, love, obedience, holiness, victory over Satan, and experience of God. Stop growing and you will start dying.

Failure, spiritual poverty, barrenness, defeat, should be intolerable to a Christian.[45] Note this however: the Christian meaning of "success" and "prosperity" does not necessarily include worldly success or material wealth; rather, it means *being successful and prosperous in doing the will of God.* The will of God for a given person may require that he amass wealth and climb the ladder of secular achievement; but for another person the opposite may be true. Yet both are required to "increase" in every aspect of their personal growth and Christian service, and in their possession of all that God has ordained for them.

David could have claimed the promise in its literal sense of building a world empire. An analogy lies there for us. Because we are the inheritors of the Davidic throne in Christ (that is, we are already sharers with Christ of that throne)[46], we too may appropriate Psalm 2:8. Not, however, to build an imperial

---

[45] Compare Jo 15:16

[46] Ep 2:4-6.

empire; but rather to build the new kingdom of God, the church. We should shake ourselves free from the "ghetto" mentality, the "remnant" syndrome, that is endemic among many Christians, and begin to think in terms (as the early church did) of winning whole nations for Christ.

Mark this: God is determined that his promises will be realized. If his own servants lack the courage and faith to possess the inheritance that is theirs, then God will give it to others who do have that boldness and zeal. Thus the history of the church is full of examples of the heathen wresting territory, wealth, authority, out of the hands of the church.[47] The same thing is happening today in our own country - the church is capitulating to secular, pagan forces. And on the personal level, individual Christians allow themselves be cheated out of the righteousness, health, prosperity, that God has promised them. They "set boundaries where God has not set them"; they allow a wrongful limit to be placed upon God's promises; they heed the devil, or their own unbelief, or their neighbor's scorn, and permit their growth and service to be restricted.

This world does not lack negative voices. They barrage every saint:

- "you cannot expect to conquer every sin"

- "some habits cannot be broken"

- "some diseases can be healed, but not this one"

- "you will never do anything great for God"

- "miracles are for some, but not for you"

- "you have gone as far as you can go, you have done as much as you can do, you have gained as much as you ever will"

- "you never will be any wiser, stronger, better, than you are now"

- and on and on the negative cacophony goes, assaulting us day and night. But you should accept no restraints except those imposed upon you by the will of God, as revealed in Scripture, or made known to you by the Holy Spirit. If no God-given boundary is perceivable, then commit yourself to limitless growth!

---

[47] One notable case; the Muslim conquest in the 7th century of north Africa, Egypt and Syria, which prior to that invasion had been almost entirely Christian. The church has never been able to regain possession of those lands.

Don't let the enemy seize what is yours! Possess your God-given territory in Christ!

HE DID NOT SEE WHAT GOD SAW

One of the great ironies of Israel's long history is that, during all that time, only one man ever saw Israel as God saw the nation - and that man was the heathen prophet, Balaam![48] He was hired to curse Israel, and probably wondered why it was necessary, given the pitiable state the people were in. But then the Holy Spirit fell upon him and suddenly he saw those tribes through the eyes of God![49]

Now, instead of a ragged assortment of slaves and refugees, he saw a glittering host, powerful as a raging lion, echoing with the shout of the King! He fled in dismay. But he needn't have worried. He was the only man there who did see Israel's innate splendor!

That failure of spiritual vision on the part of that generation cost them their inheritance in the promised land. Because they insisted on measuring themselves only by what the natural eye could see, because they refused to see themselves as God saw them, they were easily discouraged and easily overthrown. Every one of them perished in the wilderness.

Many Christians are guilty of the same spiritual folly. People who refuse to look at themselves as they are in Christ; who insist on measuring themselves by themselves, who do not give themselves a godly measure. Yet the New Testament is bold enough in what it says about the believer's position and identity in Christ, declaring us to be the righteousness of God in Christ, and more than conquerors, and able to do all things in him, and much, much more!

Do you want to grasp that "much, much more"? Then you must break past the barrier of your natural perception and learn to see yourself only as God sees you in Christ. Let your eyes be enthralled by the successful future, the continual increase that God has ordained for you in Christ! Let your heart take courage from the victories God has decreed for you in Christ!

Go back to Balaam for a moment. How different was Israel's natural aspect from the vision he saw of the people! Just as the pagan prophet looked past Israel's outer shape to the inner spiritual reality embodied in that nation, so we must penetrate the flesh and grasp the eternal truth of how we appear in Christ. It is obvious how we look to the natural eye. Ignore that view, and speak rather how you appear in God's eye (see, for example, Romans 8:30, and notice the past tense: we are *already* "glorified").

---

[48] See Nu 22, 23, 24.

[49] Nu 24:3-5, 23:9,10,21,22

Think about Jesus. The glory that blazed out of him on the mountain was always in him,[50] except that it was usually hidden within his flesh. We share a similar condition: as we walk in fellowship with him, we are changed daily into the image of the Lord, *"from glory to glory"*[51]. Learn to see yourself, to think about yourself, to speak about yourself, in terms of that indwelling glory. As a result of your union with Christ by faith, that is how God sees you; why should you see yourself any differently?

Beginning from that point, you should apply to yourself God's promise of *"much, much more"*! In some areas of your life and ministry you will be looking for physical growth, numerical increase, or material enrichment. In other areas you will be looking for spiritual increase or enlargement. In still others, you will be seeking a growing perception, a deeper understanding, a bolder appropriation - for example, you should be growing in your revelation of the glory of Christ in you, and in your ability to walk in the power of the Holy Spirit, and in your commitment to serve God, and in your comprehension of scripture, and so on.

What prevents Christians from catching this heavenly vision, so that they ask only a little from God?

A limited expectation can be caused by things like the following: fear, unbelief, sin-consciousness, worldliness, ignorance of the promise, broken fellowship with Christ or the church, guilt complex, sense of unworthiness, timidity, laziness, reluctance to allow the affairs of the kingdom to interfere with personal ambition, and so on. All such things can be used by Satan, either to persuade you that you have no right to claim the promise, or to make you unwilling to claim it. The antidote is clear enough: be done with sin, away with unbelief, stand up in Jesus' name, and begin to claim the super-abundance God has promised you in Christ![52]

But is it right for a Christian to be ambitious, to be committed to success?

To a certain kind of pious Christian the words "ambition" and "success" are obnoxious. Those people prefer to adopt a passive, fatalistic, self-negating life style that is really the antithesis of the bold and dynamic life-style displayed in scripture. Certainly we should "die" to all carnal ambition and success. But once

---

[50] Mt 17:1-2.

[51] 2 Co 3:18

[52] Notice 2 Corinthians 9:8, which is perhaps the most extravagant verse in the whole Bible. It could be translated literally: "God is able to make ALL grace <u>abound</u> toward you, so that in ALL things and it ALL times you may have ALL self-sufficiency and may <u>abound</u> in ALL good works!" Count them: there are seven superlative in that one sentence! Or perhaps you would prefer this:" God is able to do vastly more than you could ever ask or even imagine, according to his power that is at work with in you!" (Ep 3:20)

you know what the purpose of God is for your life (in the secular world, the church, and in your personal and family affairs), then you should be consumed with a passion to see that purpose richly fulfilled (John 2:17; Psalm 119:139; Titus 2:14; Hebrews 10: 7,9; Philippians 3:12-15; etc.) By contrast, the following references deal with carnal ambition - that is, committing yourself to achieve goals that are not sanctioned by God, or that are attempted without his assistance: Psalm 49: 10-13; 127: 1-2; Habakkuk 2: 5,6,9; Matthew 16:26. But I am expecting better things of you than that - things that belong to righteousness, and that will glorify God in their accomplishment!

Just as the Spirit of God opened the eyes of the pagan prophet, so he can open your eyes to see everything from a heavenly perspective. He will do this in response to earnest prayer, especially when that prayer is linked with a devout study of scripture. Those three things: the Word, prayer, and the Spirit are the key to divine revelation.

Be warned by David. When the vision of God faded from his eyes, they became engrossed by another vision, a forbidden one, that cost him the loss of nearly all that God had given him. The promise of "much, much more" depends upon seeing what God sees and pressing on to fulfil it. Any other dream will become a nightmare.

HE LOST THE HEART FOR WAR

While Nathan was reproaching David, the army of Israel was waging war under the command of Joab[53]. Where was David? Sunning himself on his palace roof[54] David was still in the prime of life. Why was he not at the battlefront? What a sorry contrast with the younger David, who had sung the exultant battle cry

> *"By my God I can run through a troop and leap over a wall ... He makes me skillful in battle, so that my arms can bend a bow of bronze ... He fills me with strength for war so that all my enemies fall down before me!"*[55]

Those days were no more. The vision of God had dimmed. Tired of battle, preferring ease and luxury, he let others do his fighting for him. Beware, lest the same war-weariness, the same softness, should overtake you. Heaven takes a dim view of such slackness -

> *"Curse Meroz, says the angel of the Lord. Let a double curse fall upon its inhabitants, for they did not come to the*

---

[53] 2 Sa 11:1; 12:26-31

[54] 2 Sa 11:2

[55] Ps 18:29,34,39-45

help of the Lord, they did not fight with him against the mighty"[56]

"Let a curse fall upon anyone who is slack in doing the work of the Lord; let all who withhold their swords from bloodshed be accursed!"[57]

When David lost his heart for war, he lost everything.

So stir up your faith, your boldness, your zeal to wage unremitting war against the enemy, until you have gained your full inheritance in Christ.[58] Never lose the heart for war! We are called to be warriors for Christ, called to possess the promises, called to build the kingdom, called to advance from glory to glory until we finally enter into our magnificent inheritance when Jesus comes.

---

[56] Jg 5:23
[57] Je 48:10.
[58] 1 Co 15:58; 16:13

POINTS TO PONDER

(1) Psalm 2:8 was a promise to the Davidic throne. It primarily applies to Christ. However, David also could have claimed it. Does it have any relevance for us and, if so, what?

(2) Do you agree that God gave to heathen kings the empire that it was actually Israel's right to possess? If so, what spiritual principle was at work and how does it affect us?

(3) In what ways do Christians "set boundaries where God has not set them"? What wrongful limits do Christians place upon themselves or upon God's promises? How can you determine where God has placed a boundary?

(4) How might you allow your spiritual enemies (instead of the promises of God) to set the perimeters of your life?

(5) What happens to Christians who lose their resolve to have all that God has made available to them in Christ?

(6) Think about how different was Israel's natural appearance from the vision Balaam saw of the people (if you have not yet done so, read the whole story in Numbers 22,23,24). Apply that spiritual principle to Christian life today. What appearance do Christians have to the natural eye? What appearance do they have to the spiritual eye?

(7) Think about the things God has given you. In what way should you apply the promise of "much, much more" to those things?

(8) Is it right for a Christian to be "ambitions", to be committed to success? If so, what form should that ambition take; how should "success" be defined? If not, what concepts should replace the notions of "ambition" and "success"?

(9) Your notes say, "The Holy Spirit fell upon Balaam, and suddenly he saw Israel through the eyes of God (Numbers 24:3-5; 23:9,10,21,22)." Is it possible for us to gain the same kind of heavenly perspective on earthly things? Can our eyes be "opened" as Balaam's were? If so, how?

(10) Challenge yourself with the question, "Have I lost the heart for war?" What does that mean? How may a Christian fail as David did? What might cause that battle-weariness? How can it be overcome? What will result if you lose a heart for war? Think about Judges 5:23; Jeremiah 48:10.

THE KEYS OF THE KINGDOM!

> *"I am giving you the keys of the kingdom of heaven; whatever you bind on earth will be bound in heaven, and whatever you loose on earth will be loosed in heaven."*[59]

What a powerful statement that is! Here Jesus presents us with the very "keys" to the kingdom of God! At once, though, we face a problem: the fierce controversy this text has aroused over the centuries. Not so much over what the "keys" of the kingdom are, but rather over who possesses them. Can we solve that quarrel here? I think so; but why not judge the matter for yourself?

WHAT ARE THE KEYS OF THE KINGDOM?

We are prone to miss the force of Jesus' words because the idea of a ring of keys creates a different mental image for us than it did for the people in Bible days. If I ask you to picture someone carrying a ring of keys, you will probably think of a jailer, a janitor, a custodian, or some similar person. Those people are very necessary to the well-being of society, but they rarely occupy positions of high rank or authority. So for us, the image of a key-bearer is that of a comparatively humble member of the community. Hence the idea of possessing the "keys of the kingdom" may not stir in you any great excitement.

But that humble image was not the picture Jesus had in mind, nor would his words have had a slight effect upon his hearers. Quite the contrary, they would have been amazed at the scope of what he was telling them. Why is that? You can find the answer in the passage of scripture Jesus was quoting. He drew his words from a story in Isaiah (22:15-23). I urge you to pause now, and read that passage in your Bible. It tells how one high official, Shebna, was demoted and banished from the palace, while another, Eliakim, was promoted into his place. Note that Eliakim was made second only to the king in rank and authority in Israel. And the emblem of his new position was a set of keys that he wore on his shoulder as a badge of office. As you read the story in Isaiah, you will realize that verse 22 was the inspiration for Jesus' words in Matthew 16:19 -

> *"I will place upon Eliakim's shoulder the key to the House of David, so that what he opens no one will be able to shut, and what he shuts no one will be able to open."*

---

[59] Ma 16:19.

The expression, "what he opens no one can shut, and what he shuts no one can open, is a vivid way of saying that, in respect to the affairs of the kingdom, Eliakim's authority was to be absolute. It had nothing to do, of course, with actual doors opening and closing. So too with the expression used by Jesus, "binding and loosing". It is foolish to press it too literally. It is primarily a colorful description of great authority, exercised in the name of the King and supported by all the might of the kingdom.

Clearly then, the phrase "keys of the kingdom" is a synonym for an exalted rank before the throne of God; it is a way of saying that the possessor of those keys has the highest conceivable authority, an authority exceeded only by God himself! Whoever holds those keys can act in the name of the Lord, having access to the splendor, wealth, and might of the kingdom of God. Whatever that person speaks in harmony with the purpose of God will be supported by all the resources of heaven. Whatever he binds will be bound! Whatever he looses will be loosed!

An illustration of this idea can be seen in the mediaeval office of Lord High Chancellor of England. He wore gorgeous robes, and various badges of rank that conveyed to him enormous authority. Or, in modern times, you might think of a highly-ranked military commander, with all his medals and ribbons. Perhaps even closer, you have probably seen pictures of a king or prince, formally dressed with a wide sash across his chest, onto which are pinned the various insignia of his titles and rank. That is the image Isaiah saw, and that is what Jesus had in mind. The "keys" are pinned to a prince's sash; they mark the wearer as the most powerful man in the realm.

That at once raises the question -

WHO POSSESSES THE KEYS OF THE KINGDOM?

This of course is the matter of greatest contention, and various answers have been given -

The Apostle Peter. In Greek there is a distinction between the singular and plural forms of the second person personal pronoun, so it is easy to determine whether the speaker is addressing only one person, or two (or more). English speakers used to be able to do the same. They could say either "thou" (singular) or "you" (plural). But now we use only the form "you", which in itself gives no indication of one or many. Which form did Jesus use? Throughout Matthew 16:17-19, Jesus used only the singular pronoun; in other words, he was speaking to Peter. Therefore some claim that possession of the keys perished when Peter died.

The Pope. Others contend that Peter had the right to convey the keys to his successors in apostolic office. Thus the Pope claims them, along with the bishops of the Roman Catholic church, and the bishops of some other communions, all of whom claim an unbroken line of ordination back to Peter himself, as the first bishop of Rome. That claim may be true: the line of succession may be unbroken (unlikely as it seems), and those worthy bishops may have a valid right to the "keys". But whether or not they have an exclusive claim upon them is another matter.

A Denomination. Sometimes a particular denomination (usually one of the cults) arrogates the keys of the kingdom to itself, and denies access to heaven to all except those who come by way of that group's teaching. We can swiftly discard such conceited folly.

The Apostles. Others argue that the keys were the property of the entire group of original apostles, and that they are now displayed in the writings of those apostles (the New Testament), which alone tell us how to gain full entrance to the kingdom of God.

None of those suggestions are satisfactory. But there is a clue to solve the problem in the first one I mentioned - the use of the pronoun. It is true that in Matthew 16:17-19 Jesus apparently spoke only to Peter. But it is equally true that when Jesus repeated his promise about "binding and loosing" *in Matthew 18:18-19, he used only the* plural *pronoun. The plural shows that he was then speaking to the whole company of his followers! And the context (verses 15-17) confirms that he included the entire church in his promise of authority to "bind" and to "loose".*

So we can say with certainty: any believer who has the boldness and faith to do so has a right to pin the keys to his/her shoulder and to stand in the rank they represent. Those keys belong fully to any person, young or old, who has come into union with Christ by faith. Every born again believer has been given the full authority in the kingdom of God that the keys signify. They do not depend upon human merit of any kind. Our rank and authority in Christ are both a gracious gift of God - just as was the case in the elevation of Eliakim. If a true believer does not hold the keys, it is only because he or she, either through ignorance or unbelief, has failed to take them up.

WHAT AUTHORITY DO THE KEYS CONVEY?

If every believer has the right to possess and to use the keys of the kingdom, why are so many so weak and defeated?

Two things in the main make the keys ineffective in a person's life (that is, will nullify his or her use of the spiritual authority vested in the keys):

- the **first** is unbelief. The effective use of these keys, like everything else in Christian life, depends upon the exercise of bold faith. The promise of God must be believed. The offer of Christ must be accepted and acted upon. Authority is worthless to those who either don't know they have it, don't understand what it means, or don't know how to use it.

- the **second** is acting outside the will of God. To say that those who hold the keys possess unlimited authority in the kingdom of God, does not mean they can do anything they please whenever they please. The keys represent the King's authority and they are effective only in the King's business; they enable their holders to do the work of the kingdom, not their own work. Their aim must be the glory of the King. They must be seeking to please him. They should take up the keys only because they know that without them they cannot fulfil the will of God.

However, for those who believe God, and are living within the framework of his will, those keys retain all their royal significance. They represent the boundless authority God has given us in Christ to speak into or out of existence whatever God has said should be created or destroyed.[60]

The specific purpose for which the keys of the kingdom are given can be summarized under two headings -

(1) THEY CONVEY AUTHORITY OVER SATAN

> *"The Beast has been given authority to wage war upon the people of God, and to defeat them."*[61]

That is undoubtedly the one verse in the Bible the devil believes with all his heart! It says that Satan has been given authority to wage war upon the church, and if he can, to overcome the saints. You can be sure that the enemy does not hesitate to act upon this God-given authority. If you do doubt it, look around

---

[60] Compare the similar picture of spiritual authority given in Je 1:9-19; 17-19; 15;19-21
[61] Re 13:7

you, and see the countless shattered, backslidden, or defeated Christians! Would that we were so bold, so effective, in using the authority God has given us!

Note two things-

(a) This warfare is unremitting

Never for a moment is the attack by the powers of darkness upon the church relaxed. There is no leave from this cosmic combat. Nor is there any limit imposed upon the devil's right to assault the church. As personified by the "Beast" in Revelation 13:7, Satan has an incontestable right *"to make war on the saints and <u>to overcome them</u>."* Just how well the devil has believed and acted upon that mandate is attested by the vast wreckage of Christian lives and of churches.

That is not the way it has to be. Whatever authority Satan may have is minute compared to what God has given us in Christ. Our enemy prevails only because he believes the word of God better than we do!

(b) Satan's surrender must be unconditional

It is destroy or be destroyed (John10:10). Nothing less should satisfy you than your complete triumph over the devil and all his works in your life. There is no room for compromise. Plutarch tells how Alexander the Great captured the mother, wife, and daughter of the Persian monarch Darius (330 B.C.). He says,

> "Darius wrote Alexander a letter, and sent friends to intercede with him, requesting him to accept as a ransom for his captives the sum of one thousand talents, and offering in exchange for his friendship and alliance all the countries on the left side of the river Euphrates, together with one of his daughters in marriage. These proposals Alexander communicated to his friends. Parmenio responded that for his part, if he were Alexander, he would readily embrace the Persian ransom. Whereupon Alexander replied, 'So would I, if I were Parmenio!'"

Alexander knew that if he compromised he would lose all. As it was, he went on to win all, including the entire Persian empire. That should be your heart. Nothing less should satisfy you than Satan's absolute and unconditional surrender. There is no room for compromise. Never be content with merely partial victory. Some is never good enough. It must be all!

So often people stop short of inflicting full defeat upon the enemy. For example, they are content with gaining pardon of their sin but do not insist on being rid of it; or they are pleased to get at least a partial healing of some disease, so they stop praying; or because there is a good flow of blessing in the church they no longer struggle for true revival. But we should never be satisfied with less than the total salvation expressed by the psalmist -

> *"O Lord, my enemies are many, and those who rise up against me are numerous. Many foes keep telling me, 'You will not find any safety in God!' But you Lord are my covering shield, you are my glory, you enable me to hold my head high; as often as I cry aloud to the Lord, he hears me from his holy mountain!"*[62]

(2) THEY CONVEY AUTHORITY TO APPROACH THE THRONE

How few Christians really grasp the position and authority God has given us in Christ! Yet those who hold the keys have the right to enter the throne room whenever they please, and to stand next to the King himself!

There is a fine illustration of this in Genesis 41:38-44, which tells the story of a slave who was taken out of prison and elevated to the highest rank in the land. The slave, of course, was Joseph. Pharaoh took him, dressed him in costly robes, hung around his neck a gold chain of high office, put the king's signet ring upon his finger, made him viceroy and gave him authority over the entire land of Egypt. Notice how Jesus' words about "binding and loosing" *go right back to verse 44. Notice also verse 40, where Pharaoh gave Joseph an authority second only to his own* -

> *"You shall be ruler over all my household, and every person will do exactly what you command; only in regard to the throne will I rank higher than you do ... I am the Pharaoh, but without your consent no one in Egypt will so much as lift up a hand or a foot!"*

Put yourself in Joseph's place. Try to get a sense of the position he now held, and the right it conveyed to him. Then transfer that to today. All that is said of Joseph is true of the rank and authority God has given you in his kingdom in Christ. "I am Pharaoh," said the king, "but you will rule in my name." Here is delegated authority. The monarch conveyed to Joseph the full authority of his crown. That is what God has done for us in Christ!

Those who hold the keys of the kingdom possess an unrestricted right to come before God. Whatever lies in the purpose of God for you, you can speak into

---

[62] Ps 3:1-4

being with an authority that should tolerate no denial. The same idea is expressed in different terms in Hebrews 4:14-16; 10:19-23.

How can you join the company of those who enjoy such extraordinary access to God and such matchless authority? There is only one way: know who you are and what you have in Christ, and begin now in Jesus name to live it out in the grace of God. Discard every suggestion that the exercise of spiritual authority depends in any way upon reaching some personal level of righteous achievement. Sin in one's life, of course, must be dealt with. But God's method of handling sin is simply to repent of it, confess it, put it under the blood, and then at once continue to walk as one who is utterly righteous in Christ.[63]

CONCLUSION

Some travelling Jewish exorcists once tried to cast a demon out of a man *"in the name of Jesus whom Paul preaches"*[64] The demon replied, *"Jesus I know, and Paul I know; but who are you?"* Then the demoniac fell upon the seven exorcists and beat them so severely they ran naked out of the house howling with terror. Notice that arresting phrase, "Paul I know!" Once when I was called to deliver a demonized woman I found her locked in her bathroom crying over and over, "Ken Chant is coming; don't let him near me!" She herself did not know I was there, but the demon did. Her husband and I persuaded her to unlock the door, I prayed for her, and she was wonderfully healed by the name of Jesus.

For me, the best part about the incident was the discovery that my name was known among the denizens of darkness! Is that true of you? It should be, because Jesus has given you the keys of the kingdom!

Together then let us seize those keys and in the royal authority of Christ take dominion over all the powers of darkness, at the very throne of God joyfully claiming every good thing he has promised. Holding the keys of the kingdom you can do all your God has given you to do, receive all he has given you to receive, become all he has called you to become; you can possess your possessions; you can move mountains in Jesus' name!

---

[63] 1 Jo 1-8-12; 2:2; 2 Co 5:17-18,21
[64] Ac 19:13-16

POINTS TO PONDER

(1) How does Isaiah 22;15-23 clarify the meaning of Matthew 16:19?

(2) Express in your own words the meaning of Isaiah 22:22.

(3) What is signified by the phrase "the keys of the kingdom"?

(4) On the matter of who possesses the keys of the kingdom, what importance can be placed on Jesus' use of the second person personal pronoun?

(5) Do you have a right to the keys of the kingdom? How do you gain that right? Have you possessed them?

(6) What may nullify the effect of the keys?

(7) What limits are placed upon Satan's right to make war upon the saints?

(8) What should your attitude be toward the devil?

(9) How much access do you have to the throne of God?

(10) Are you among those "whose names are feared in the corridors of darkness"? How does one join that company?

REIGNING AS KINGS!

> *"If, because of the sin of one man, death reigned over everyone, how much more will those who receive God's abundant provision of grace, and his gift of righteousness, reign in life through the one man Jesus Christ."*[65]

What an arresting statement! God calls us to reign as kings in life! Here is no permission to cringe, grovel, or crawl through life, but to live as a monarch should live. Here is an invitation to walk with royal authority, to stand tall before God, to have an abundance of all that we need to do the will of God. We are to be the men and women God has called us to be, fulfilling all he has called us to achieve, reigning as kings, lacking nothing, possessing everything! Paul says we are to be full of the joy of the Lord, seated upon the throne of our God, strong against sin and temptation. Are you trampling all over the kingdom of darkness, laughing at the oppressions of the enemy and scornful of this world and its presumed strength, which in relation to the strength we have, is nothing at all? If not, you should be!

Does that seem too good to be true? Does it seem too far removed from the lowly experience of most Christians? Your doubt should be dispelled by a striking contrast Paul makes. He says there was a time when, through one man's sin, *death* reigned over us. But now he says that through another man's righteousness we reign in *life*.

The first man, of course, was our forefather, Adam. Because of Adam's sin, death has reigned over all the children of Adam; that was his gift to us. You didn't want it, but there was nothing you could do to avoid it. Just being a child of Adam made you the slave of death. You know how real that bondage is, for you have felt the powerful sting of death, yet you were helpless to escape it. Despite what you thought about it or whatever you might have chosen to do about it, you were obliged to accept Adam's gift of slavery and death..

But now, Paul says in contrast, another man has come along, and through his righteousness, and through the abundance of his grace, he has given us *his* free gift, which is not death, but life. That man is Christ, who has turned Adam's gift

---

[65] Ro 5:17. This chapter is a transcript of a sermon I preached in San Diego, California, in 1985.

around, so that just as surely as sin once reigned over us in death, now in Christ, we should reign in life.

Did you notice that the same principle applies both to Adam and to Christ? Slavery to death came to you as a *gift* from Adam; reigning in life comes to you as a *gift* from Christ. You can't earn your royal authority, there is nothing you can do to deserve it; nothing remains except to recognize that this kingly state comes to you freely by the grace of God. As surely as being a child of Adam made you the slave of death, so now that you are a child of Christ, you are the monarch of life through his gift to you. His gift! As far as God is concerned, you are already equipped to reign in life; he has already made this true of everyone who truly believes in Christ.

Yet Paul is still not content. I would find it wonderful enough if he had said only this: *"As through one man's sin death reigned over us, so now, through the other man's righteousness, we reign in life."* But he makes it even more marvelous. He expands it: *"If through one man's sin, death reigned over you, how much more through this other man's righteousness, will you reign in life."* He wants you to grasp how real this experience of Christ's life and of Christ's royal authority should be! Measure how well you felt the sting of death and sin. You hardly need me to help you do that. Cast your mind back over the years and you'll soon recall all the times that you were tyrannized by sin; all the times that death worked its corrupting work in you. You know how strong those enemies are. Yet Paul insists that *much, much more* you should experience the impact, the strength, the sheer limitless energy of the life of Christ!

Much more than sin ever reigned over us, we should reign over sin, and not just over sin, but in all of life, so that we are the slaves of none, neither man nor devil. We are God's freeborn children, blessed by his name, called to reign in the authority of Christ!

What a sad contrast there is between the apostle's description of what Christian life ought to be and what we often observe. How many Christians do you know of whom it could be truly said, *"There is a person who is reigning in life, living like a king through all the changing circumstances of each new day"*?

We look around and commonly see Christians who are no freer than their ungodly neighbors; Christians who are as worried as any unbeliever, just as anxious, troubled, perplexed, bothered and bewildered as the unrighteous are - sometimes more so. They can't find a way to be happy in heaven or hell. They are miserable in both places.

Why is this so? Why do so many fail to experience the *"much more"* of the victorious life that Paul says should characterize all of us who once were slaves to sin and death?

No doubt there are many reasons, and I suppose those reasons vary with each individual. But here are three things that are essential precursors to enjoying the quality of life that scripture says is the prerogative of every child of God.

CONFRONT YOUR HIDDEN FEARS

Hidden fears are the single greatest enemy to the possibility of you reigning in life. Fear! No foe is more paralyzing to spiritual vitality than fear. No enemy is so devastatingly destructive to faith as fear.

I once took a count, and discovered there are no less than eighty places in the Bible where the formula is stated, *"fear not, believe only"* - not always in those exact words, but the idea, fear and faith in opposition to each other. Before you can *"believe only"* you must learn how to *"fear not"*. Notice he did not say, *"believe only"* and then you will *"fear not"*, but the reverse. Faith itself is not an antidote to fear. You can't overcome fear by trying to believe, because while fear is there you *cannot* believe. Faith is impossible where fear is allowed to remain resident in the human spirit. Before you can *"believe only"* you have to learn how to *"fear not."* That means you must uncover the hidden anxieties, the secret dreads, the dark frights that haunt the corridors of your mind and spirit. If you want faith to overcome sickness, you must at least be rid of the fear of sickness; if you want faith to prosper, you must first be rid of the fear of poverty; and so on.

Often people want to believe in healing because they are afraid of sickness, or they want to believe God for prosperity because they are afraid of poverty. Being afraid of something is not a proper motive for believing God. You cannot construct faith on a foundation of fear. If you are afraid of something it will stop you from believing God - you won't get victory over that sickness; you won't gain the prosperity you hope to receive from the Lord; you won't enjoy victory over sin; you won't be able to embrace the righteousness of Christ, or live a victorious life, or reign as a king in life. You must first confront every hidden fear. Bring them out to the light! This is the antidote to fear; not faith, but courageous confrontation of the things that fill you with dread.

When my sister and I and our younger brother were little children our parents often took us to the beach. We would walk along the shore, lifting up rocks, turning them over, trying to find crabs. The tingly thrill of our search was not finding a crab, but the terror that we *might* find one. We didn't really want to expose a crab; we hadn't the faintest idea what to do when one did scurry out, which happened from time to time. The real excitement of it was coming up to a rock and digging our little fingers underneath it, never knowing just what might be there. Suddenly we would tip the stone over, then jump back, in case a whopper might be under there with a great claw - snap, snap, snap! I still remember the delicious thrill in that adventure. For us children it was probably an important lesson in how to confront fear; we were learning how to expose the things we were afraid of. Walking up boldly to the thing that made us afraid, throwing back its cover, compelling it to rush away when its dark hiding place was opened up to the bright sun, taught us courage.

Somehow, when they reach adult life, many people lose that boldness to face their fears, so they try to cover up the things that frighten them. They try to bury them under worship, or faith, or the promises of God. They hope that on a foundation of fear, they can build confidence and trust in the Lord. But you cannot do this. The only foundation for faith is faith. Fear is no foundation for faith, on the contrary, fear undermines faith.

So before we can believe, before we can hope to enjoy this incredible joyous life Paul talked about, we must bravely walk up to our fears and throw off their camouflage. We must learn to toss away the cover-up, to compel every fear to stand under the scrutiny of God, confronting each one boldly, picking them up, tearing them out of our spirit, and casting them away.

You may say, *"Why do you preach like this to us?"* Because I know that many Christians are engaged in a great fear cover-up. They are afraid, but they won't admit it to themselves, they won't admit it to God, they won't admit it to their neighbor, they won't admit it to their spouse, but they are afraid. Of what? Afraid they will lose their health and be sick; afraid they will lose their job and be reduced to poverty; afraid some important enterprise won't succeed; afraid they never will get victory over the habits that dominate their lives. Afraid that, in the end, the devil, the flesh, or the world, will win. Afraid they never will receive the abundance in life that Christ wants them to enjoy.

If you are in that state, turn over those rocks; make those crabs scuttle away! Don't let fear find any resting place in your heart. The first step to reigning as kings is to confront your hidden fears, and the second is to

CONFESS YOUR NEW IDENTITY

Many people live with low self-esteem. The present system tends to make them feel they are worthless. This poor self-image makes them worried about whether they are liked or disliked; so they need constant reassurance. They are convinced, if they see two people talking over on one side of the room, *"They're talking about me, and what they're saying has got to be nasty. It can't be nice."* These timorous souls think the worst of themselves; they know they are not liked, not wanted, not appreciated; they give themselves no value.

Perhaps it was the way they were brought up; perhaps their parents treated them with such disdain or indifference that an impression was deeply wrought into their spirit that they really are just a piece of garbage borne on the flood tide of life. Perhaps they failed in their career, or through the shattering pain of divorce their sense of self worth is gone. Perhaps a business enterprise collapsed and broke the back of their confidence, leaving them discouraged, despondent and dispirited. Perhaps its the way their spouse treats them, or the way their children treat them. Who knows? It could be a combination of many things; but the result is the same. They may be Christians, but they are far from reigning in life!

We often look at ourselves from the human viewpoint. If I look at myself with only my own eye, or look at myself only through your eyes, then I would have to say what a worthless piece of tissue this ambulating corpse is. But scripture challenges us not to see ourselves through our own eyes, or through the eyes of our neighbor, *but only through the eyes of God.*

What does God think about me? Let me listen. Do you know what I hear God saying? *"I like you; you're a nice person to know."* That too is what he says about you!

I can't remember the exact occasion, but I can remember about the time I first made that discovery. After spending years imagining that God could hardly stand the sight of me, that I was a spot on his beautiful fabric, and that given half a chance he would take the roughest, most abrasive cleanser possible, and scour me right out of existence - after years of thinking that way about myself, I finally made this incredible discovery: *God actually likes me!* He wants to be my friend, and wants me to be his friend. He is willing to trust me with some of the most priceless treasures heaven possesses. A mark of true friendship indeed!

The Lord says, *"I have loved you (Ken) with an everlasting love."* [66]Do you know what happens when you find that God loves you, even likes you? You find a few good reasons to like yourself. Then suddenly you think that everyone else likes you too.

I tell you honestly, it always surprises me to learn that someone doesn't like me. That's a shock to me. I can't believe it! How can anyone not like me? My astonishment does not stem from pride or conceit; it is simply an inescapable consequence of the discovery that God likes me. If you know that God likes you, is your friend and trusts you, you gain a wonderful new identity. What a marvelous thing that is! Suddenly you begin to like yourself, you come to like everybody else, and you expect them to like you.

All of this is a product of what Christ has done for us. For, of course, the man God likes is not Ken Chant, the son of James Oswald Chant and Vera Gwenneth Chant; no, the man God likes (and that I now like) is the new man in Christ - the

---

[66] Je 31:3

new Ken Chant, who has been given a new identity as God's son, God's servant, God's friend in Jesus.

Suppose you have a low self image. How are you going to respond to this common human infirmity of being afraid of your neighbors, afraid of what they are saying about you, convinced that no one really appreciates you, that no one really likes you? There are three ways to respond to this. One is to do nothing about it. You could continue to wallow in self pity for the rest of your life. If you choose to do that you will never reign, you will never know the full dimension of Christian experience the scriptures describe.

Of course the whole reason for this writing is not to leave things as they are, but to say, *"today is going to be different."* How are you going to make it different?

The second approach you could take is to go out and seek much good advice from the many counselors who are very willing to give it. This world is full of good advice.

I noticed something for the first time in the newspaper yesterday. I suppose I had seen it many times, but this time I realized how ironic it is. It's from the El Cajon newspaper, *The Daily Californian*. Every day they have one page devoted to comics and to other columns, such as *Ann Landers* and the like. This is the heading from that page: *Comics and Advice*. That suddenly struck me as an ironic conjunction. If I were Ann Landers I think I would disapprove of that association of my advice column with comic strips!

However, unconsciously that ironic heading does express a certain truth. People rush here and there, everywhere seeking advice, asking for counsel, looking for some new solution to their problems, some new psychological insight. They bustle here and there, read this or that popular author, go to one psychotherapist or another. Yet all the time, what they really need is not more good advice but a revelation of the Word of God. Compared with the solution God offers to our dilemma, even the best advice is on a par with a comic strip!

If the people of God had the revelation of scripture they should have, they would think of themselves better than they do. You would hear them confessing their new identity in Christ, not their old one in Adam.

When I talk about this man, Ken Chant, I do not talk about a man born of human parents, but a man born supernaturally of his Heavenly Father, by the Holy Spirit, through the name of Jesus Christ. That's who I am, and that's who you are too! After I began working on this message, I came across this song -

> **"Blessings and more blessings overtake me,**
> **All his commandments I observe;**
> **While my soul doth prosper in the knowledge**

> **Of Jesus Christ my Lord, the living Word.**
>
> **That's what I have, that's who I am.**
> **I am a king come out of Abraham.**
> **Because of Christ, I reign in life in him.**
> **That's what I have, that's who I am."**[67]

"That's what I have, that's who I am!" God's new man in Christ, called to reign in life! This brings me to the third option: confess your new identity. We all have two identities: that of the "old nature", born of Adam; and that of the "new nature", born of Christ. Therefore we all have this choice, day after day: which of those two identities will you grasp? One of them has to become the theme of your faith-confession. You can say, *"I know nothing but defeat, failure, despair, fear, unbelief. I am a sinful, corrupt, broken failure!"* Or you can say, *"I am a child of the King; his nature is in me; his word is my strength; his promise is my joy; I can do all things in Christ!"*

You can pick the first confession if you want to. You can speak as though you have no other identity except that of a child of Adam. You can put yourself right back into the first part of our text, which says *"by one man's trespass, death has reigned over all."* You can go back there and stay there if you want to, and accept Adam's gift to you of death and defeat, ignoring Christ's gift to you of kingly authority. If you do, you will remain a slave to sin and death.

Better you should pick the second confession! Put yourself into the second part of the text, numbered among those who choose to receive the gift of righteousness and the abundance of God's grace and to reign in life in Christ. If you make that choice you can say, *"What do I have? Everything! Who am I? God's royal priest in Christ! That's what I have, that's who I am!"*

Through Jesus Christ we have been brought into the covenant that God made with Abraham. Because of Christ we reign in life, in him. That's what we have, that's who we are. That has to be your confession, not just here in church, but Monday, Tuesday, Wednesday, Thursday, Friday, Saturday, and again Sunday.

Confront your hidden fears; confess your new identity; then there is a third key to reigning in life -

---

[67] David Ingles; David Ingles music, Tulsa, Oklahoma; 1978

CONFIRM YOUR ROYAL AUTHORITY

Wherever I go I see Spirit-filled saints in church on Sunday morning, shouting, singing, rejoicing, saying *Amen*, and having a great time. But no sooner do they walk out of the church, than the balloon goes down. Victory is gone. It's back to the same old grind of anxiety, uncertainty, temptation, fear and defeat. Dear friends, I don't want to *preach* about a new reign in your life, I want to *see* it! This is not just doctrine, its reality. We should be *doing* this. This is how we are called to live. It is not just a joyful text for a cheerful sermon. We are called to reign in life in reality, and to stomp the devil underfoot.

Christ is looking for a church full of victorious saints, not a group of sinners that are only half saved. There is work to do for the Lord, but it can't begin until Christians seize their real authority and begin to speak with kingly majesty, taking command over all the works of the kingdom of darkness.

Again we face a choice. Let me illustrate it with a story about Alexander the Great and his incredible conquests in the fifth century before Christ. Empires and kingdoms fell under the yoke of Alexander. In his march of triumph and terror, he finally came to the ancient city of Sidon in Phoenicia. He subdued Sidon and dethroned its king, Straton, because he had refused to surrender at Alexander's demand. Having banished Straton from Sidon, Alexander commissioned his general Hephaestion to find a new monarch to rule over the city in Alexander's name.

The general made inquiries, and found a relative of the royal family living in the suburbs of Sidon, in very humble circumstances. He heard a good report of this man, who was reputed to be a man of integrity and honor, though poor. Let me read now from the history of the Roman historian, Quintus Curtius -

> "(Hephaestion) decided that no one was preferable to a certain Abdalonymus, a man who had, it is true, a distant connection with the royal family, but who, because of narrow means, was cultivating a garden in the suburbs at scanty profit. The reason for his poverty, as is true of many men, was his honesty, and intent as he was on his daily toil he did not hear the din of arms that had shaken all Asia. Unexpectedly then (the messengers of Alexander) came with the insignia of the royal dress into the garden, where, as it chanced, Abdalonymus was engaged in clearing up, by plucking out the useless weeds. Then, after hailing him as king, one of them said, `You must change that mean garb of yours for the apparel which you see in my hands. Wash yourself, stained as you are by the filth and dirt of the earth, take on the spirit of a king and carry on your self control into that fortune of

which you are worthy. And when you sit upon the royal throne, master of the life and death of all the citizens, do not forget the condition in which - nay, by Heaven! because of which - you are receiving the crown.' It all seemed to Abdalonymus like a dream. From time to time he kept asking whether those who were so saucily making sport of him were altogether sane. But when, as he hesitated, the dirt was washed from his body, and a robe adorned with purple and gold was put upon him, and the good faith of the messengers was confirmed by oaths, now a king in earnest, attended by the same (courtiers), he entered the royal palace."[68]

What a striking story that is, and how well it illustrates the position in which we find ourselves. There we were, scrabbling around in the dirt of this world, trying to pluck out a few weeds from the tainted soil of our lives. There we were in squalor, poverty, and misery, until the King of kings sent a messenger to say, *"You are chosen to reign as kings in my name."*

People sit in church, listen to the sermon and say, "It doesn't work, it's not real, it isn't true. It might work for others, but it doesn't work for me. Maybe the preacher can get up there, onto the throne, but I can't. Leave me here among my weeds. Leave me here in my dirt patch."

Just like Abdalonymus. It seemed to him like a dream. It seemed to him that they were making fun of him. But even as he hesitated in unbelief, they washed the dirt off him, put the robe on him and hailed him as king. They said, *"Abdalonymus, come and take your throne."* They said, *"TAKE UP THE SPIRIT OF A KING."*

Doesn't that touch something in your spirit? Can't you hear the Holy Spirit saying to you today, "How long are you going to stand there with bowed heads and soiled hands? How long are you going to grub around in the mud patch of your earthly life? How long will you cling to those soiled robes? How long before you let me wash the dirt off you and put the robe of royal authority on you? How long before you take up the spirit of a king, and begin to tread on serpents and scorpions, and over all the power of the enemy? How long before you cast off sin, destroy sickness, deliver the demon possessed and grasp the riches of the blessing, grace, and goodness of your God and Father?"

All of this, said Paul, belongs to us in Christ. It is God's gift to us in Christ. It comes to us - as the royal authority came to Abdalonymus - not *despite* our lowly condition but *because* of it! It results from the Father's grace. It is made ours

---

[68] I have a Photostat of this story, but no details of the volume from which it came.

solely by our union with Christ through faith. There is nothing to do except to believe it and to begin to live it.

May God then give us boldness to *confront our hidden fears*, to *confess our new identity* and, this day, to *confirm our royal authority*. May you walk from this day forward with the spirit of a king, reigning in life in Jesus Christ our Lord!

MOUNTAIN MOVERS

> *"Jesus strongly emphasised this saying: 'If you banish all doubt, and speak only with faith, you will need merely to tell this mountain to be shifted from where it stands, and thrown into the sea, and what you command will be done. Indeed, you will be given anything you ask for in faith!'" (See Matthew 21:18-22)*

Christ invites you to take the initiative, and through the exercise of spiritual authority to reshape your world. He says that God has given you the right to determine the shape of your environment. You can change your situation! You can alter your destiny!

With incredible boldness, the Lord declares: "Whatever you ask in prayer you will receive, if you have faith." *Whatever? Yes, whatever you ask, you will receive!*

Can those words be taken seriously? Surely it is not possible to believe that such impossible things can be done?

There are two extreme reactions to this "mountain-moving" promise of Christ:

- there are those who say that it promises nothing;
- there are those who say that it promises everything.

The first group treats the promise as a pious metaphor, arguing that it relates only to victory in the spiritual realm. They emasculate the words of Christ and reduce prayer to a religious exercise. The second group treats the promise with exact literalness, insisting that it means precisely what it says. They use it to encourage people to demand from God anything and everything they want.

Both extremes fail. The first because it asks too little; the second because it asks too much.

Some Christians ask for too little. They argue that it is improper for a devout believer to "take the initiative". They insist that we must accept the things that happen to us, meekly allowing God to do whatever he pleases.

Other Christians ask for too much. They fail to recognize that some events we cannot alter, and that in some situations the Father himself demands only humble submission to his will (Matthew 26:39-44).

We need to find a place of balance. For example: there is always room, even in the darkest valley, for a believer to be bold in faith and to seize some special grace from God (Psalm 23:4-5; James 1:2-4; I Peter 4:12-14, etc.). Beyond that, there are other circumstances, which the Father has put under our own control, where he expects us to take authority and to change what is happening (compare Matthew 6:30; 14:31; and Mark 4:35-41, where there is an implied rebuke of the disciples because they had not themselves taken authority over the storm. Note that Jesus had already given them his word that they would reach the other side - verse 35. On the strength of that word they should have defied the power of the storm to drown them that night.)

We need to learn, then, how to handle Jesus' "mountain moving" promise in a way that retains its vigor but keeps within the purpose of God. I hope these pages will help you to do just that.

MOUNTAIN-MOVERS HAVE A DISCIPLINED SPIRIT

Implicit in Jesus' words about "mountain moving" is the idea that you possess a spiritual power called "faith" and that the disciplined use of this faith can make the impossible possible. You can get an idea of what this means from I Thessalonians 5:23 -

> *"May God make you and keep you perfectly sound in your entire spirit, soul, and body."*

Notice that we are composed of body, soul, and spirit. Three things can be said about each of these parts of our nature -

   (a)   They each have a unique mode of expression

   ♦   the body expresses itself through energy and action

   ♦   the soul expresses itself through thought and feeling

   ♦   the spirit expresses itself through belief and worship

   (b)   They are all unceasingly active

   ♦   your body and soul are never wholly at rest; they never come to a place of complete inaction; there is always some movement, thought, feeling, expenditure of energy.

- likewise your spirit is always at work fulfilling its role of belief and worship.

The human spirit is compelled to believe something, and it cannot help but worship something. The question is not whether you are believing and worshipping, but what are you believing, who are you worshipping?

Have you ever realized this? Every moment of every day, you are believing something and worshipping something. It is no more possible to stop your spirit believing and worshipping than it is to stop your heart beating. We have only the choice of determining what we are believing, and who (or what) we are worshipping.

    (c)   They must each be brought under control

Just as you recognize the need to discipline your bodily actions and to restrain your thoughts and feelings, so you must recognize the need to bring your spirit under control. That is what Jesus meant when he said, "If you have faith..." *He was talking about the believing power of the human spirit. He demands that you seize control over that power and channel it toward the promise and power of God. That is "faith" as distinct from "unbelief".*

Notice that "un-belief" is not "non-belief". No human spirit can ever be in a state of "non-belief", but only in a state of right or wrong belief. That is, you are not free to stop believing, for your spirit is incessant in the exercise of its believing power. You are free only to choose how you will use that power, whether rightly or wrongly; whether toward the promise of God (which the Bible calls "faith"), or away from the promise of God (which the Bible calls "unbelief").

Because of our fallen state, our spirits, if left alone, will always worship and believe the wrong thing. It takes an act of will, of steadfast training and discipline to compel the spirit to maintain an attitude of unwavering faith. Just as our bodies, our thoughts, our feelings, if they are left unrestrained, will go rampant and quickly bring us to physical, mental, or emotional ruin, so the ruin caused by an uncontrolled spirit is no less awful.

Notice also that "faith" and "unbelief" represent an exercise of exactly the same believing power. Only the direction in which that power is turned has changed. It takes the same spiritual energy to believe wrongly as to believe rightly. Just as a car uses the same engine to take it forward or reverse, depending upon the driver's choice, so you must choose to bring your spirit under control and to direct its believing power toward God.

Never forget this: a condition of "non-belief" is impossible. I must say it again: "unbelief" is still a state of "belief" - that is, of believing that the promises of

God cannot be trusted, of expecting evil things instead of good, of anticipating failure instead of success, and so on. Unbelief represents an expenditure of spiritual energy as great as that required by right belief (or faith), and it leads to negative results just as dramatic as the positive results produced by faith.

There is no neutrality here. You are believing something right now: either to get well or to remain sick; to overcome sin or to be defeated by it; to succeed or to fail; to rise to prosperity or be reduced to poverty; to receive good things from God or bad things from the devil; to be changed into a better person or to remain just as you are - and so on. At this very moment the believing power of your spirit is either taking you toward God or away from him; either toward the fulfillment of God's promise to you, or away from it. The choice is yours.

No wonder Solomon said: "Keep your heart with all diligence, for out of it flow the issues of life" (Proverbs 4:23). The things your life will produce are ultimately determined, not by anything that happens in the outside world, but by what is happening in your own spirit. You must compel your spirit to maintain an attitude of faith. Don't allow it to stray from the promise of God. Be vigilant! Lock your expectations onto God, anticipating nothing except the things that come from his hand.

No outside person, thing, or event has any final power over you. The ultimate issue of each person's life is determined within himself or herself. We alone choose whether we will react to each happening with faith or fear, trust or doubt, love or malice. We alone determine whether our enemies finally do us harm or lift us closer to paradise!

Mountain-movers have a disciplined spirit!

MOUNTAIN-MOVERS EXPECT GREAT THINGS FROM GOD

When Jesus challenged his disciples to start moving mountains by faith, he showed two things:

First, their expectations were too small.

They were astonished because he had killed a fig tree simply by speaking to it (Matthew 21:18-20). He was astonished at their astonishment and he rebuked them. Their faith was too little. He insisted they learn that God was willing to do greater things for them than they had dared to dream.

Does it surprise you that a tree will obey a man when he tells it to die? Perhaps you, too, need to open your ears to Christ's rebuke. We are all of us far more likely to annoy God by the pettiness of our pleas than by the greatness of our requests!

Second, everything yields to spiritual authority.

This is probably the greatest lesson hidden in this incident. Christ was trying to teach his disciples the irresistible power of spiritual authority. Nothing can withstand it. If you understand spiritual authority, two things will follow:

(a) You will act, and not be acted upon.

You will always know how to seize the initiative, and at the very least bring every circumstance into spiritual conformity to the purpose of God (compare Genesis 45:4-8; 50:19-20). In many cases you will be able to change the very circumstances themselves (compare 2 Kings 1:9-10).

No matter what your circumstances may be, there is always some kind of spiritual initiative you can take. Consider Jesus: when it was appropriate to do so, he passed through the mob and would not allow them to capture him (Luke 4:30; John 8:59; 10:39). When that was no longer possible, when by the Father's will he had to yield to their murderous hands, he still kept his spiritual mastery (John 19:11; Luke 23:34; Matthew 26:53-54). See also Colossians 3:22-24. Notice that Paul is presenting this challenge: can a man who serves another voluntarily and heartily be any longer a slave? He may be one outwardly, but inwardly he is now a free man.

So the rule is this: if it is right for you to act with spiritual authority and to change what is happening (as when Jesus hushed the storm, healed the sick, rode the untamed ass, and so on - and compare Mark 16:15-20) then you should do so in Jesus' name; but even when that kind of overt authority is not permitted by God, you should still take an inner spiritual initiative. You should never in any circumstance surrender spiritual mastery. You should never be merely acted upon.

The entire life of Christ is an example of this. By the use of spiritual authority he subdued storms, turned aside the howling mob, fed the multitude, calmed the insane, drove out disease and demons, and so on. Even when he was finally taken by his enemies, he still kept spiritual mastery over the situation so that in his very death the purpose of God was fulfilled.

In other words, Christ was never merely acted upon. Rather, he was always himself the centre of the action. He never for a moment yielded into another's hand the control of his destiny. By faith he absolutely overcame the world and compelled it to do his will (I John 5:4; and compare I Peter 2:21).

(b) You will succeed and not fail.

Jeremiah is a good example of this principle. God told him that failure would be impossible for him if he would but stand firm in his God-given authority (Jeremiah 1:9-10, 18-19). God did not promise him a life of easy comfort. On the contrary, he was warned of hardship and fierce opposition. But he was promised success. He would be invincible. Mighty nations would rise and fall at his word. The authority of all heaven stood behind him. He could not fail.

For you, too, if you understand and use spiritual authority, failure is impossible, success is sure.

Is it really proper for a Christian to be totally committed to success so that the possibility of failure becomes absurd? It is improper to have any other attitude! See John 15:16; 2 Timothy 4:8; I Corinthians 9:24-27; Hebrews 10:36-39; and many other references.

Every mountain moves away from those who boldly expect great things from God!

MOUNTAIN-MOVERS SUBMIT TO THE WORD OF GOD

At this moment I have no confidence that I could move a million tons of rubble just by speaking to it. Why not? Because I have received no personal word from God that would give me the right to do so. The rule is this: true faith cannot exist apart from a word from God. *You can speak into existence only what God has given you personally the right to speak.*

That means, you need to hear what God is saying in each new situation. Your word has irresistible authority only when it harmonizes with the word of God; you can achieve the impossible when you attempt only what lies within the parameters of the Father's purpose.

So you must give yourself to the task, day by day, of hearing from heaven, of discovering God's specific promise, his particular purpose, for you today.

Remember also that God says different things to different people.

Read Hebrews 11:32-38. Notice the list of unconquerable mountain movers, mighty heroes of faith, men and women who wrought stupendous miracles in the name of their God.

But notice also those who were destitute, naked, hungry, hunted, who dwelt in caves, who were tortured and murdered, yet who were also "well attested by their faith".

They were all men and women of faith because they had all heard from God and were obedient to the word that came to them from heaven, whether that word spoke poverty or riches, life or death, miracle or martyrdom.

Faith, then, is a believing response to something God has told you, and it includes an absolute resolve that the word God has spoken will be fulfilled in your life. Faith brooks no denial of that word. Faith is determined to have all that God has promised, to do all that God has commanded. That kind of faith can move any mountain that blocks the promise of God.

POINTS TO PONDER

(1) What are the two extreme (and erroneous) ways of handling the promise of Matthew 21:18-22? Why are they wrong?

(2) Is it proper for Christians to "take the initiative"? Shouldn't we rather yield before the things that happen to us, meekly allowing God to do whatever he pleases?

(3) What are the three parts of human nature? In what ways do each of those parts express themselves?

(4) Can the human spirit ever stop "believing" or "worshipping"?

(5) Is it possible to be in a state of "non-belief"?

(6) Ask yourself: "What am I believing at this very moment? In what way is my spirit exercising its believing power?"

(7) The principle expressed in Proverbs 4:23 is immutable. How is that principle being worked out in your life? For good or ill?

(8) Is it possible to come to the place where "you always act and are never merely acted upon"? What does that mean? How could you apply that principal to your present circumstances?

(9) Is it proper for a Christian to be totally committed to success so that the possibility of failure becomes absurd?

(10) What "mountains" do you have the right to move? What things are you able to call into existence simply by speaking the word?